HAPPILY **NEVER** MARRIED™

Odessa,
Glad you can
join in this celebration.
I trust you will find
some message that
resonate with you.
Best, 5/21/17
KH

HAPPILY NEVER MARRIED™

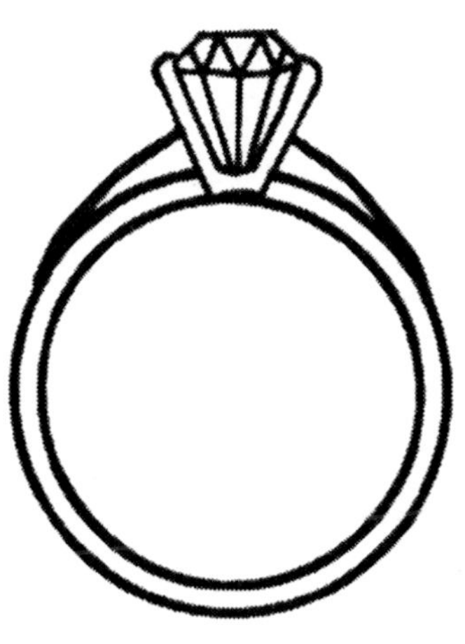

Kendra L. Harris

Copyright © 2016 Kendra L. Harris
All rights reserved. No part of this book shall be reproduced, stored in a retrieval system, or transmitted by any means, electronic, mechanical, photocopying, recording or otherwise, without written permission from the author, except for the use of brief quotations in a book review.

ISBN: 0998245003
ISBN 13: 9780998245003
Library of Congress Control Number: 2016917310
Happily Never Married LLC, Huntsville, AL

DEDICATION*

This book is dedicated to: my parents **Rebecca and Daniel Harris** (deceased); my aunt, **Esther Harris Clemons** who for my entire life has been like a mother, aunt, and sister to me; my brothers and sisters-in-law, **Dr. Joseph L. Harris, Tyrone and Pamela Higgins Harris, Mark M. Harris, and James (Jay D) and Mayor Lillie Thompson Martin**; my nephews and nieces, **Jose and his new wife Nicole Ortega Harris, Michael Jones, Jaron Harris, Joseph Harris, Matthew Harris, Micah Harris, and Brian Martin_(deceased)**; my never-married fabulous cousins: **Linda Carlos, Bridget Coates, Cheryl McElveen, Sylvia Murphy, Valerie Harris, and Monia Trusty;** my younger never-married cousins, **Nia Brown, Briana Harris, and Airiana Carlos-Lee**; my cousins who have taken particularly good care of me **Mamie and Michael Minor, David Harris, Jerry Coates, Jon Wilson, and Al & Beverly Carter**; some of the best friends a girl could have **Lanta Evans Motte & Charles Motte, Jr., Solomon Irwin Royster, Eldridge (Roddy) Allen, and Monique & Kelvin Raeford;** friends who continually propelled this overall project from its beginning, **Dr. Gary Reynolds, Kondria Black Woods, Brian Alford, Derrick Davis, Cynthia Johnson, and Melanie Cooke;** my goddaughter and her brother, **Angelina-Rose Raeford** and **Aqel Amede;** and extended family members, **Kimberly Harris, Almetrice "Metrice" Page, Rev. Beatrice Royster, Toni Harris, Cheri Harris,**

---

* **Disclaimer:** I know it was very risky for me to "name" so many names in my dedication and acknowledgments. Unfortunately, there is a great chance I have forgotten people who very likely should have topped the lists. Please forgive me. I will have to make it up to you in my next book!

Yvette Smith Harris, Keith, Keenan, and Morgan Thompson, Le'Undra and JaLence Hunt, Senia White-Hunt, Jaylen, Bryten, and Damon Hunt, Rosalyn Raines, and Danielle Kittrell.

This book is dedicated to the *seasoned* individuals in "my" village: Ernest Harris, Herbert and Mary (Edna) Harris, Ramona Wilson, Steve Coates, James and Jerome Jackson, Josephine Page, Verline Perry, Delores & Clarence Bennett, Sister Mary Brenda Motte, Vivian Davis, Dorothy Corpening, Elizabeth Norwood, and Carrie Williams. A special dedication also goes to all the family members who rest under the branches of the Jackson, Harris, and Martin family trees; my adopted Evans family in Florida, the children, grandchildren, and great-grandchildren of **Louise and Obediah (OB) Evans (deceased);** extended family members; and those who have transitioned from this life.

This book is also dedicated to my "Atlas Neighborhood" family: Those family names include: Allen, Anderson, Beale, Bradshaw, Brown, Cox, Davis, Dawkins, Glenn, Gross, Harrison, Hepburn, Hill, Holt, Howard, James, Johnson, Jones, Mangana, Means, Perry, Smith, Stevenson, Tucker, Void, and Wyles. A special dedication goes to those who kept a watchful eye on my parents: **Curtis Perry, Edith Holt Smith, Zina, Chanell, and Stepfen Glenn, Vincent Price, Cecilia Bradshaw, Daryl Davis, and Norman Clark. I also solute the wonderful neighbors I have had across the years including: Dr. Jeffrey and Monica Moore Holmes, Pat and Greg Oglesby, Kim and Kerry Wilson, Rosalind Harper, Persephone and Whit Deas, Nancy and Tom Cantwell, and "Truck."**

Finally, this book is dedicated to those women whose actions and works helped to create a world in which I was afforded the *option* to live the life I am living.

CONTENTS

ACKNOWLEDGMENTS

Thank you to those who had a direct hand in the look and feel of the book: Dr. Andrea Tillman Hawkins, Rodney Funderburg, Sabrina McMickens Tanner, Padraic Major, Princess Carter, Shana Michelle Hereford, Coya'Lyn "Lyn" Corn, Joy Thomas Moore, Lamar Braxton, Tammi Cochran, and Dana Harris.

Thank you to the coordinators of the first book signing – MBA 507 Class - Fall 2016: Ashante Anderson, Tonjelynn Baldwin, Tavaris Battles, Octavia Brown, Chassity Burns, Monique Charleston, Isha Conteh, Nina Darby, Tavoris Hall, Tyveisha Hall, Janaisha Hayes, Maleeka Hollaway, DeWayne Kendricks, Torin Malone, Meredith Minor, Melvin Payne, Christopher Sledge, Tierra Stegall, Sha'Retha Williams, and Jasmyne Winfield.

Thank you to the "Never Married" research study contributors – MBA 507 Class - Fall 2015: Shirley Alexander, Tia Bailey, Tenathius Bassett, Gina Battle, Aneka Billings, Courtney Calvin, Ramone Campbell, Charlotte Canady-Slater, Jessica Coleman, Jonathan Collins, Terry Dent, Tiffany Donaldson, Edward Faust, Meshanda (Judy) Fitcheard-Hagood, Alexandra Harris, Reba Jasmin, Juanita Lackey, Belinda Love-Washington, Cleveland McCall, Cande McDowell, Quentin O'Cain, Britney Pean (deceased), Princess Pelmer, Karshella Purifoy, Nicole Richardson, Terriell Springfield, Roberto Turner, Brandon Willis, and Simone Young.

Thank you to the millennial focus group: Michael Allen, Darrell Compton, Montez Gordon, T'keyah Gully, Desmond Harrison, Charese Howard, Caleb Hood, Austin Jones, Angel Richards, Kylan Riley, Dymond Spells, Shannon Stewart, Skylar Taylor, and Christopher Thomas.

Thank you to those who helped to give this concept its wings: Harold Fisher, Candace Adkins, Raymond "More Better Man" Woods (deceased), Dr. Audrey B. Chapman, Stacey Little, Dr. Charnetta Gadling, Dr. Robert Brown, Dr. Jim Harper, and Keren Johnson; Chapters of Delta Sigma Theta Sorority, Inc.: Nu Alpha Chapter (American University, Washington, DC), The Federal City Alumnae Chapter (Washington, DC), Western Wake Alumnae Chapter (Apex, NC – [Raleigh/Durham, NC vicinity]), Huntsville Alumnae Chapter (Huntsville, AL), and Central North Alabama Chapter (Madison, AL); and WHUR (Howard University Radio).

Thank you to those who have supported my overall endeavors: Dr. Benjamin and Janette Newhouse, Donna Brown, Terry Bankston, the Honorable Gerald and Edna Vincent Lee, Bernard Gregory McNeal, Cynthia Lindsey McMickens, Adrienne Benton, David Byrd, Arthur J. Horne, Jr., Wiley Mullins, Jan Harris, Dr. Peggy Lee, Angela Dixon-Van Croft, Dr. Darryl Banks, Acie Ward, Dr. Sybil Henderson, Brett Chambers, Jackie Brown, Randal Rogers, Dr. Vanessa Perry, Dr. Leila Borders, Dr. Gail Ayala-Taylor, Dr. Jacqueline Williams, Dr. Charles Richardson, Jr., Dr. Geraldine Henderson, Dr. Marilyn Liebrenz-Himes, Rev. Dr. Richard and Bridget Soles Hayes, Dr. Donna Grant, Emily Page, Alisa Tami Johnson, Davetta Dunlap, Dr. Cassandra Atkinson, Jonica Roland, Phyllene Washington, Dr. Teresa Merriweather Orok, Mrs. Yvonne Thomas Stevenson, Dr. Del Smith, Dr. Larry McDaniel, Dr. Barbara A.P. Jones, Dr. Helen Gabre, Mrs. Yvette Clayton, Carlton Joyner, Delisia Matthews, Elizabeth Shareef, Adrina & Rahmud Bass, Ruby Tonnette Artis, Anteea Janel Green, Stacia Parker Ross, Tyrone Simmons, Nicole Chestang, Thedis Bryant, Dr. Kendra Minor, Dr. Pauletta Bracey, Drs. Sundar Fleming, Mary Phillips, Dierdre Guion,

Cameron Seay, Cindy Love, Berkita Bradford, Alisha Malloy, Sharron Hunter-Rainey, Judy Siguaw; Rob Chapman, Chandra Tedder, Brenda Parker, Deborah Brame, Mona Pittman-Moore, Maceo Caudle, and Ritchie Cherry, Sr.; my friends and colleagues from, Alabama A&M University, Howard University, North Carolina Central University, the PhD Project, Ford Motor Company, and the National Black MBA Association.

Thank you to my forever village: Lynne Ridley Harris, Monica Moore Allen, Bari Edgehill, Donna Hampton-Lewis, Renee Kent Harrison, Stephanie Holley, Farnese Haynes McDonald, Cynthia Lomax, Delia Small Millet, Edna Olive, Shelly Scott, Patti Spady Ross, Cynthia Spencer, Janice White Taylor, Paula Commodore, Dr. Jennifer Durham, Delavay Osborne Miner, Monique Osborne, Anntoinette White Richardson, Carol Waters Allen, Joanne Saunders Brooks, Phillip A. Lattimore, III, Donald & LaShawn Vaulx DeVille, A. Donald McEachin, Alexis & Felix Yeoman, Bernadette Bullock, Van & Deborah "Ross" Crawford, Rev. Steve Tillett, Rev. Joseph & Madelyn Daniels, Rev. Timothy and Paula Curry Warner, Andre & Susan Craig Robinson, Reggie Williamson, Gwendolyn Murphy Corbitt, Maurice Brooks, Dr. Willie Jolley, Eric Hood, Robert Bailey, Wayne Tyler, Steve Hughes, Wanda Lucas, Hugh Watkins, Quintin Adams, Jon Blue, Brian Harris, Cecilia Grillo, LaJoy Mosby, Gregory Harrod, Cheryl Davis, Eugene Cox, John Young, Lisa Miller, Oscar Mardis, Kim Wilson, Dargeelyn Loftin, Dr. Lionel Thomas, Karen Coleman, Sonya Scott, & Arthur Edmunds.

Thank you to my "H" town people: Susie Briggs, Bonnie Butler, Claire Camp, Traci Carpenter, Alesia Carter, Raven Griffin, Tamela Hammond, Kirsten Hardware, Yvonne Holley, Joanna & Raymond Kidd, Glenda McLaurin, Tamaron Middleton, Al Mitchell, Norma Oliver, Ethelene Purnell, Pam Stuckley, Karen Taylor, Bobby Teague, Tinola Teague, and Jackie Thurman; **and my Zumba ladies:** Tanisha and Laquieta Austin, and Wendy Jones.

INTRODUCTION

THERE IS SOMETHING HERE FOR EVERYONE

THE SHOCKING REALITY of the state of marriage (or divorce) in the United States is that the divorce rate is greater than 50 percent for first-time marriages, 67 percent for second marriages, and 73 percent for third marriages.[1] Hence I felt somewhat vindicated as an older, never-married individual when a few years back, a network television Sunday morning news segment reported that females older than fifty who have never married are the happiest individuals in the United States, rivaled only by *happily* married couples. In fact, in 2014, the percentage of Americans who had never married was 30.4 percent, up from 22.1 percent in 1976. Furthermore, the rate for divorced, separated, or widowed individuals increased to 19.8 percent from 15.3 percent.[2] Therefore, more than 50 percent of Americans are single. That means that single individuals are now the majority!

As a member of the older, happy, and single demographic, it has become increasingly apparent to me that although the current state of marriage in the United States is unenviable, the perception of my life as an older, never-married female is often negatively stereotyped. That to me is a contradiction. The reality is that I am living my life and

1 Mark Banschick, "The High Failure Rate of Second and Third Marriages," *Psychology Today*.com, February 6, 2012, https://www.psychologytoday.com/blog/the-intelligent-divorce/201202/the-high-failure-rate-second-and-third-marriages.

2 Allison Schrager, "Most Americans are Single and They're Changing the Economy," Bloomberg, September 15, 2014, http://www.bloomberg.com/news/articles/2014-09-12/most-americans-are-single-dot-what-does-it-mean-for-the-economy.

enjoying it. I have not allowed my "single" (and in my case "never married") status to be an impediment to my happiness; however, US society often wants to portray me as lonely, miserable, and perhaps undesirable. Hence there is a need to lend a voice to the dialogue of understanding who we older, single individuals are, and moreover why getting married is often not the panacea it is often painted to be. Let me be clear that this book does not espouse that marriage is an undesirable status. Divorce is undesirable. To the contrary, under *authentic* circumstances, marriage appears to provide for a beautiful existence. However, there are immeasurable conditions and circumstances that, in general, are often not taken into account when people contemplate marriage. Older, never-married females are one group, it would seem, that has tended to incorporate those conditions and circumstances into their considerations regarding getting married. I had always told myself that marriage for me was something that I wanted to do only once. Since I have yet to identify the optimal relationship dynamic that is right for me, one that would provide a quality of married life that is acceptable, never being married has been a source of happiness.

I, like countless never-married older women, started out dreaming of my wedding day that would come along in my twenties, followed soon after by having children. (A research project I supervised with an MBA class at Alabama A&M University concluded that often, never-married older women have actually been engaged multiple times. I myself have been officially engaged once, and strongly urged to consider engagement a second time.) As we older women transitioned from idealistic adolescents and young adults into practical-thinking women, and our individual experiences and wisdom grew, our thinking on the subject of marriage evolved. In my case, although I have maintained the desire to be in the "happily married" group, I have a clear understanding of the practical reasons for why I am not there "yet."

The aforementioned circumstances have led me to write this book, a collection of essays authored by me. The essays cover a variety of subjects that have formed the tapestry of experiences and observations that have resulted in my being "happily never married." In this book, I introduce themes that represent the challenges and realities I have experienced and observed in finding the "right" person to marry, and in observing others who have sought marriage or are married.

Recognizing that cynics might perhaps say that since I have never been married, I am in no position to provide commentary on the state of marriage in our society, I say to them, clearly, most Americans would likewise then be considered unequipped to do so, given the atrocious divorce rate. Hence I provide a perspective that has prevented me from becoming a divorce statistic. Quite frankly, my thirty-plus years of observations and experiences as an adult illuminate issues that occasionally cloud others' thought processes because our society seems too often to insist that getting married is the only option for living a happy life.

Although the genesis of this book (my blog of the same name) was in large part based on my desire to give voice to older females who have lived a life similar to mine, as I continued to develop the essays for this book, it became very clear that the themes are universally applicable when it comes to the subject of marital status. Hence I trust most individuals who read this book will find aspects of it that resonate with them, irrespective of their gender, marital status, age, or culture.

The essays in this book are for the most part independent of one another. Although the theme of any given essay ties into its chapter, which ties into this book's overall theme, the individual essays are largely free-standing. Hence this book need not be read in any sequential order. Therefore, I encourage you to select an essay title that is particularly interesting to you, read that essay, and repeat that pattern with other essays herein. In the couple of instances whereby an essay has either a substantive connection to another essay, or kinship with an essay somewhere else in this book, the associated essay is indicated. Enjoy!

PART 1

KEEPING IT REAL

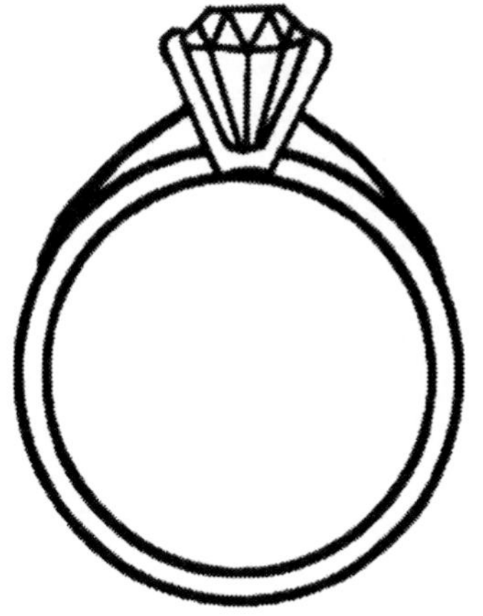

ESSAY 1

SETTING THE RECORD STRAIGHT: THE RIGHT TO "CHOOSE"

My parents (now deceased) lived to see their sixty-eighth wedding anniversary a few years ago. This fact was an understandable source of pride for my parents; my siblings; me; and legions of family members, friends, and associates. On the day of their anniversary, I posted a picture of them with my brothers and me on my Facebook page and announced their anniversary. In this same posting, I also announced that I was writing the "Happily Never Married" blog.

As would be expected, the post yielded a multitude of well-wishes to my parents on the occasion of their anniversary. Two readers out of forty-five made mention of my blog being a great idea. (I think the blog announcement in general got overshadowed by the anniversary.) One reader (ironically not one of "my" Facebook friends), posted the following: "Congratulations to your parents. Now when you start getting sick, and old, and lonely, you made the choice to be alone."

I will not belabor the point of the obvious rudeness of the post, surpassed by the fact that this individual was not an intended recipient. (Remember, she was not one of "my" Facebook friends.) Instead, I will focus on how the sentiment expressed in her post in many ways represents the essence of my motivation for this book.

Let me first reiterate the thoughts I express when addressing my "never-married" status. I have wanted to be married since I can remember knowing what marriage is (perhaps since age five). My desire to be married has never waned, and I am happy for all those married couples that are authentically, happily married. I certainly would not argue that my single status is a choice; however, that choice is not born out of a desire to be alone, or left alone. It is born out of a practical understanding that maintaining a healthy marriage is something that most Americans who have tried it have miserably failed (note the 50 percent divorce rate for first-time marriages and higher rates for subsequent marriages). Hence I have made the choice to proceed cautiously when it comes to getting married.

Let's consider the part of the Facebook comment that notes I would be "...sick, and old, and lonely." Anyone older than fifty is already considered "older." I am neither sick nor lonely. There are countless individuals who are lonely in a relationship. To me, that is the worst kind of heartache. I have been unfulfilled in relationships whereby I was not receiving the level of companionship that is most optimal to me. Although the termination of a relationship is quite painful, the feeling of being free to pursue the type of companionship that best suits me is quite liberating.

Being lonely has no age limit. Being sick has no age limit. When people live their lives in a way that is giving and supportive of others, they will receive love and support in their time of need. Conversely, if they live a more selfish, self-absorbed life (or marry someone with those characteristics), they may find themselves devoid of support when needed. Personal character, rather than marital status, will be a determinant of fellowship and love. I certainly acknowledge that conventional wisdom suggests that a spouse or children who have healthy familial relationships provide the best love and support for one another in times of need. However, having a family of procreation (spouse and children) is no guarantee of support in times of illness or loneliness, especially if the person needing it is of poor character, or the person who should provide it is of poor character. Unfortunately, there is no dearth of older individuals in need of someone to care for them who are, or were once, married.

ESSAY 2

THE "TOO PICKY" FALLACY

IN A COUNTRY where the divorce rate is greater than 50 percent for first-time marriages, 67 percent for second marriages, and 73 percent for third marriages, never-married females older than fifty recognize many of the issues that have created these statistics.[1] We also recognize that any endeavor (i.e., marriage) that touts such an abysmal set of odds for success would be avoided by most people if it were any other endeavor. At the very least, a cultural practice (marriage) that has such a high failure rate warrants some dissection.

One place to start the analysis is to look at why people have gotten married in the first place. At a basic level, we fiftysomething singles have escaped many of the "real" reasons people have gotten married. As a society, we have become desensitized to some of the reasons that many people get married in the first place, including the following:

- All their friends are getting married.
- They are enamored by good looks, money, or power.
- They want to flee from their parents' homes.
- They fall in love (or so they thought) with a childhood sweetheart (only to learn that they became much different people as they grew older).
- Their families are pressuring them.
- Their biological clocks are ticking.

---

1 Mark Banschick, "The High Failure Rate of Second and Third Marriages," *Psychology Today*.com, February 6, 2012, https://www.psychologytoday.com/blog/the-intelligent-divorce/201202/the-high-failure-rate-second-and-third-marriages.

- They are pregnant.
- A fling turns into a ring.
- They are on the rebound.
- They do not want to be perceived as undesirable (old-maid syndrome).
- They think they will never find another person.
- They fear being alone.
- They think they can change the person they are marrying.
- They get married at a contrived time ("insert wife here").
- They just plain settled!

These rationales for getting married all too often are the genesis of a failed marriage. Unfortunately, many of us who recognize these conditions as the essence of faulty reasoning are often characterized as picky, unrealistic, and demanding. We contend that if the choice of a mate is one of the single most important decisions people can contemplate regarding how they live the rest of their lives, our general discretion, scrutiny, practicality, and plain old common sense should be applauded, not perceived as picky.

I offer numerous facts to be considered when people find themselves quick to characterize a never-married individual as "picky." First and foremost, never-married individuals recognize that any one person's accommodation or compromise in choosing a mate is another person's deal breaker. In other words, there are people who will marry a person with a particular (undesirable) characteristic, while legions of other people would label that characteristic as a deal breaker. This holds true for practically any characteristic one might consider.

As an example, some women accept as a basic premise that men are largely incapable of being monogamous. Hence, these women will find ways to be content with a womanizing husband, as long as the husband brings his paycheck home. Other women would find this accommodation totally unacceptable, however being accepting of a man who is unwilling to maintain steady employment but does not "stray." Each one of these women might declare that they absolutely would not be involved with a mate who had the characteristics of the other woman's mate. Fiftysomething females who have never married, would likely say that neither man is a major "prize" and would more often opt not to become involved with either of them, and hence subsequently be described as "too picky."

ESSAY 3

A WOMAN'S BEST ACCESSORY?

(Inspired by a blog comment from Cynthia Johnson)

ONE OF THE visitors to my blog (a precursor to this book), "Cyn," commented on a post that talked about single women being too picky. One of the things she wrote was that when she bought her second house, a single-family home (moving from her previously purchased townhome), someone said to her that she (Cyn) must not want a husband.

The sentiment behind the comment made to her is indeed a sad testimony. Instead of everyone rejoicing over Cyn's real-estate acquisition, at least one person obviously viewed her purchase as being symbolic of the stereotypes with which single women are often subjected. This brought to mind that some of the actions we take as women are often interpreted as our defiance of traditional male-female roles in relationships.

What makes Cyn's experience even more frustrating is that many men complain that they do not want to be pestered by "gold diggers." So, let me see...some men do not want to see a woman amass her own wealth. Some men complain about gold diggers. The woman who is amassing her wealth is the opposite of a gold digger, but she still has problems because her wealth generates a set of negative assumptions about her need or desire for a man or husband.

The experience Cyn had reminds me of a statement made by a female hosting a Saturday afternoon television movie feature. She stated that, "A woman's best accessory is a man on her arm." Although I interpreted that her statement was meant to be tongue-in-cheek, there is a reality to the sentiment.

On hearing the television personality's declaration, it occurred to me that if part of my desire was to someday be married, I had gone about my life completely wrong, starting with my perception of the benefits of my accomplishments vis-à-vis coexisting in a relationship with a man. I had always assumed that the better I prepared myself to exploit my talents and develop positive attributes (i.e., good character, good education, good career, wealth accumulation), the more attractive I would be to a male. It turns out that although "some" men might appreciate my preparation, other men are turned off by it.

As opposed to my accomplishments being viewed as assets that I bring into a potential union, my accomplishments work against me. For some, my accomplishments are viewed as a challenge to a man, or a declaration of my insistence that I do not need a man, instead of a demonstration of my desire to join with him to create something together that is bigger than the two of us independently. I consider this to be a sad testimony. So it appears that my premise of being fully capable of "pulling my weight" in a relationship, and bringing valuable resources to the relationship, is a premise that is diametrically opposed to many men's philosophies and views of what they want in a spouse.

It would appear that my positioning, relative to a man, is what's desirable. It starts with having him on my arm, which shows that some man desires me; therefore, other men's interest in me is heightened. Ironically, I recall that some married women and some pregnant women have indeed validated that sentiment. That is, some married women and pregnant women have articulated that they attract as many if not more men with the visible signs that they are already attached (i.e., a wedding ring, being pregnant). This inherently signals that some man somewhere found them desirable, which often results in other men being drawn to them (and I do not mean on a platonic basis).

If that game is going on, it is no wonder that the state of marriage in America is in such disarray. I always subscribed to the notion that first and foremost, two individuals need to be fully unattached in order to be in a position to have a relationship. Furthermore, I generally followed the tenet that I did not want to "take sand to the beach." In other words, if I was attending a function where single men would be present, I would not want to show up with a date, thus looking like I am already taken. Hence too often, in my strategy to attract "unattached" men, I unwittingly went about it without my best accessory—a man on my arm.

ESSAY 4

SACRIFICE VERSUS DUTY: A WOMAN'S BURDEN

When I was writing my blog, a reader, "Cassandra," commented that single women *and* married men are the happiest among us.

This comment evoked my thoughts regarding what *seem* to be the sacrifice(s) that women are often expected to make in a marriage. There is certainly the adage that men fear marriage because they do not want to sacrifice their freedom. However, one of the outcomes of many marriages appears to be that women make the greatest sacrifices. To that end, census data confirm that men are more likely than women to remarry (presumably, in part, because men gain more than they sacrifice).

From 1950 to 1989, the rate of remarriage overall declined. However, without exception, more men remarried than women.[1] A relatively recent article describing some women's sentiments on this issue stated the following, "It's fun being a girlfriend. A wife? Not so much. Cooking, housework, and juggling multiple schedules is exhausting—and many women feel they were doing it as a solo act, giving 90 percent to someone else's 10 percent."[2]

It seems that women are often the ones who are expected to subordinate their goals, wants, and desires for the sake of their husbands and their families. Although healthy marriages are characterized by ongoing

---

1 Rose M. Kreider, "Remarriage in the US," Annual Meeting of the American Sociological Association, Montreal, Canada, 2006.

2 Jill Brooke, "Marry Again? Nine Reasons Divorced Women Choose Not To," More.com, December 16, 2009, https://www.firstwivesworld.com/index.php/resources-articles/item/5076-marry-again-nine-reasons-divorced-women-choose-not-to.

mutual sacrifices and continuous negotiations, in countless other marriages, women are making exceptional sacrifices. For example, women often put their education and careers on hold. Women are generally the "trailing spouses," deferring to their husbands' career advancements. And women are the ones who more often experience "skill-set atrophy" (a stunting or decline in their professional skills) because the education and talent they possessed going into a marriage aren't always leveraged to their fullest ability within the marital structure. Hence postdivorce, these women must find a way to retool in order to reenter the workforce. Seldom, if at all, do you hear of men who have had to reassess their skills or retrain as a result of divorce in order to become employable.

These issues brought to mind an experience I had many years ago as a newly minted "MBA" fresh out of a well-respected business school program. I became acquainted with a would-be suitor who asked the proverbial question, "What do you do [for a living]?" I proudly described my Fortune 500 corporate position in sales and marketing, to which he replied, "When I start my business, you can be my secretary." Sadly, he was not joking.

Let me be very clear that I recognize that society overall has come a long way in just the past twenty years alone in regard to respecting a woman's talents, and that the level of ignorance described in my experience, fortunately, does not apply to most men. I also recognize that the issue of divorce is a complicated one that cannot be reduced to a single factor. However, the ongoing vestiges of some of the archaic ways in which women have had to sacrifice to keep their marriages intact, I believe, is one of the reasons why some women who make the exodus from a marriage are not interested in repeating those nuptial vows again.

Kudos to those men who have recognized the holistic value in their wives and have worked to make their marriages as reasonably equitable as possible for their families as a whole. And bravo to those women who have created a formula that optimizes both the professional and personal aspects of their talent in a way that keeps their marriages harmonious. Both roles take hard work and concerted effort.

ESSAY 5

EMOTIONAL SUPPORT: HEARING *AND* LISTENING

I CANNOT COUNT the number of times I have explained issues to customer service representatives only to have them give me a response that is not commensurate with the issue at hand. After repeating myself a few times, I generally come to realize that they might have "heard" me talking but they were not actively "listening" to what I was saying. The manifestation resulted in the misdiagnosis of my issue, and therefore, an inappropriate response.

This reminds me of interactions I have had with individuals on a personal level, and in particular on a romantic level. I experience and witness all too often that most people do not "listen." They might have perfectly functional hearing, but their listening skills are subpar.

One of the most frustrating aspects of a romantic interest not "listening" is that when you pour out your heart, you get a response of cluelessness, indifference, or what feels like an abrupt change in subject. The emotional result is one of feeling like you have been left dangling off of the side of a cliff. The positive aspects or just plain indication that one has been listening is that there is engagement in the content of the conversation. For example, if someone walked into a room and said that there was a terrible car accident outside and that if the victims of the accident were not dead, they have clearly been hurt, one would expect that the receivers of this information (if they had an ounce of emotional quotient) would follow with a series of questions. The questions might flow something like the following: Are emergency vehicles on hand?

Are emergency vehicles on the way? Do we need to dial 9-1-1? Can you tell when the accident occurred? (Did the accident just happen, or had the accident taken place before the informant arrived, suggesting that emergency personnel are already on hand?) If emergency personnel have not yet arrived, is there anything that can be done to provide assistance to the victims?

What one would not expect is to walk into a room, announce such a travesty, and be met with a nonresponse or other form of outright indifference to the scenario that has been painted. Unfortunately, this brand of indifference or lack of engagement is exactly what too many people face when they are sharing a part of themselves with someone (particularly a romantic interest). One can imagine that if one had shared the news of such a real-time travesty taking place near someone's front door, some sort of a reaction that indicates empathy, heart, and caring for one's fellow man would be expected. At the very least, one would expect the people at the gathering to show concern for the well-being of the messenger, an eyewitness to a travesty, understanding that although that person was not personally involved, he or she might be experiencing some emotional distress.

In interpersonal relationships, how often do we leave the communicator hanging? How often do people bear their souls or share something painful only to be met with indifference or some other sign of lack of engagement? How long or often do you think people can be met with such indifference before they become drawn to someone else who does provide that emotional support?

Many of the ills of relationships could be solved by simply listening. Listening can lead to humane responses that draw people to you. The lack of listening can have the opposite effect. It can push people away.

ESSAY 6

HIS LAST NAME

As mentioned in another essay, I was engaged a while back (essay 42: "The Unengaged: A Secret Society"). Being the youngest and the only girl in my family, there was a range of emotions from my family when I was preparing to be married.

Clearly my father was someone at the top of the list of individuals who weighed in on the subject. I was not surprised to discover that my otherwise low-key, unassuming, even-keeled father did have a sentiment with respect to my impending nuptials. What I was surprised about was what that sentiment was.

I was marrying someone who was ten years my junior, who had political ambition, and whose hometown was three thousand miles away from where I was raised, and where my parents and most of my siblings resided at the time. In light of all of that, my father's biggest source of trepidation was that I was going to be losing my surname, Harris. (For the record, I was engaged during a time when women often kept their maiden names, and I had not determined with certainty, or discussed with my father, what my decision was with respect to how I would handle my last name vis-à-vis getting married.) To be perfectly honest, the subject of my new last name became one of my main considerations as well. Truthfully, I cannot recall whether the power of my father's suggestion placed these thoughts at the forefront of my consideration, or whether the trepidation was previously there. I recall, and continue to realize, that a name change symbolically reconstructs the person from their former self. Kendra "Smith" is a human entity that is foreign to Kendra "Harris." Furthermore, unless society has created some omnipresent, prescient e-mail that magically corresponds with everyone who has ever interacted with me, informing them that Kendra "Harris" is no more and should be replaced with Kendra "Smith," the name change is like a rebirth under an alias that is unknown to the masses. Even though there would be witnesses at the wedding who would be knowledgeable of the name change, they would likely forget the new surname two minutes after the "I dos."

The generic "wife's new last name decision" and my father's sentiment regarding my name with respect to my impending marriage are issues that have occupied my thoughts to varying degrees practically my entire life. Long before I ever became engaged, I had once determined that if I were to marry, I would hyphenate my last name so that I could honor the heritage of my family of origin (and maintain some semblance of my existing identity), while also celebrating the acquisition of my life mate. However, at some point I realized that this technically meant I would have a different last name than that of my spouse (Kendra Harris-Smith and John Smith).

I then decided that I would drop my middle name, replacing it with my maiden name, and use my married name as my new surname (Kendra Harris Smith). But then I realized that with this option, if people were looking for me, they would have to know to look for "Smith," because "Harris" would not come up in search results or in an index.

This indirectly brings me to one of my latest iterations on the subject. At some point, it occurred to me that if and when I do get married, I will marry the "one" for me, my optimal mate. In that regard, taking his name will not be a source of trepidation or sense of lost identity, but instead will be a tremendous source of pride and celebration. Let me emphasize that this is a sentiment I have for me, Kendra Harris. It is a decision that I have contemplated for decades and for which I now have peace. I must emphasize that what brings another woman her peace is for her to decide. That decision should need only the negotiated result of communication with her future spouse. It is not the business of anyone else. As a matter of fact, I reserve the right to change my mind on the subject again if the time comes!

ESSAY 7

IN THE HOUSE

This essay is dedicated to my parents [now deceased], my family, and the individuals who grew up in the Atlas neighborhood in northeast Washington, DC.

When I was in elementary school, one of my mother's colleagues advised my mother that if she continued to raise her children in the neighborhood in which I grew up, those children would amount to nothing. Today that neighborhood is part of the trendy, highly sought-after, upscale real estate in our nation's capital. At the time I was growing up there, the neighborhood was simply "the hood," suffering from post-1960s riot blight. For the record, my mother's colleague was not someone who was an elitist who looked down her nose on humanity. She was simply a product of the culture in which we live, one that all too often is hung up on facades and clichés as opposed to being focused on what lies within. In her heart, my mother's colleague was being a good friend and advisor to my mother. My mother responded to her well-intentioned colleague by saying, "I don't raise my children in the street, I raise them in the house!" For the record, my mother and father (both high school educated) have raised and supported children and other family members (in that same house) who have had great successes in life. Among this group of offspring and wards are doctors, lawyers, educators, and entrepreneurs. What's more, the families on my block were solid citizens who have made immeasurable contributions to society.

The advice my mother's colleague gave her is reminiscent of the fallacy we succumb to when evaluating individuals for being a potential mate. We look at external armor and clichéd facades as opposed to examining what lies beneath; in other words, we neglect to investigate what's "in the house."

The transformation of my neighborhood is a great metaphor for the evaluation of a mate. If one bases a relationship on what seems trendy, what happens to that relationship when that trend goes out of style? Today's visitors to the neighborhood in which I was raised are enamored by the renovated row houses, businesses that have relocated to the neighborhood, and the "professional crowd" that makes its way to the neighborhood almost every evening to indulge in happy hour, dine, or simply hang out in one of the new game-oriented establishments that have proliferated. (Note: When my parents first moved there, prior to the 1960s riots, the neighborhood had thriving businesses.)

How many women this very hour are trapped behind the majestic double doors of a lavish house in the "right" neighborhood only to emerge in the light of day, hiding the scars of the beatings they get from their husbands at night? Does the fresh paint of a newly renovated home in a "trendy" neighborhood cover up relationship woes behind closed doors? The "complexion" of the environment might have changed, but have those changes made its households immune to relationship woes? We sometimes make positive assumptions about people's character and, therefore, their suitability for a relationship based on superficial images.

Conversely, we make negative assumptions based on stereotypes, and we make judgments based on trendy standards. The facades of buildings *and* individuals will be ever changing; however, the core of those things and people are undeniable. If we are attracted to one another based on who we *truly* are, then we're in it *together*. We will thrive off of that power of two, and irrespective of what's going on with the façade, all will *truly* be well "in the house." I want a genuinely loving relationship based on authenticity and truth, not on beauty and wealth. Sometimes the house that shelters an "authentically" loving relationship needs a paint job.

Sometimes the house is dirty, and sometimes the grass needs to be cut. But at all times, the house with the genuinely loving couple is one that is safe, peaceful, and welcoming. When we base our relationships on what's trending or what looks good, the quality of those relationships will ebb and flow like an ever-transitioning neighborhood.

ESSAY 8

PENISES AND PETRI DISHES

One of my favorite shows that was introduced on television in the spring of 2016 was, *You, Me, and the Apocalypse.* Essentially, the main concept of the show was that life on earth as we know it was going to be destroyed in a few days or so. As a result, as one would imagine, mass chaos was breaking out across the world.

Part of the story line also included that some government officials had established the proverbial doomsday bunker, which of course could accommodate only a few chosen, privileged souls. A key aspect of the establishment of this bunker, and the ensuing stewardship over its inhabitants, was the essential need to establish a way forward for the continuation of mankind. In that regard, there was one species that was essential in its organic form—a healthy, fertile female.

It was apparent that obviously in order to preserve the human race, the conception, gestation, and birth of children were a nonnegotiable part of the strategic plan of human preservation. The revelation in this plan was that sperm can be harvested and stored. A human egg can be extracted, fertilized, and stored. However, the gestation of a child at this point in our evolution has no substitute. It must be organic. Nothing takes the place of having a healthy, fertile woman to actually carry an embryo to its time of birth.

Knowing this to be a fact of life calls into question how it is that as an American society, we have devolved in many aspects to have limited respect for women, too often relegating them to second-class status. Women are the undisputed vessels for furthering life. How is it that our society has gotten to the point where such a treasure is routinely cast as second class, seemingly always in a fight for equal rights and the respect that has been justly earned?

The lack of respect and honor for women as the essential vessels for furthering life is often manifested in relationships. Conversely, men (more importantly, their penises) in a doomsday scenario could be depreciated down to the worth of a petri dish.

Make no mistake, playing a caste-system game for any reason, even for the rationale of saving humankind as it exists, is a proposition that goes against my spirit. However, if a true worst-case scenario were to come to pass, a sperm bank, some petri dishes, and real, live *women* would be all that mattered.

ESSAY 9

YOUR SPOUSE CAN'T ESCAPE WHO YOU ARE

As someone who has been a university professor for numerous years, one thing I continuously witness is students struggling to determine what they want to be when they grow up, and parents (or other influential adults) exerting pressure on exactly what that should be. One thing these observations have shown me time and time again is that in the final analyses, people are apt to excel, thrive, and live happy lives when they pursue their passions. (Listen to any motivational speaker, and you will hear that they echo this sentiment.)

Most of us (I dare say all of us) have a passion, talent, or skill within that we need to leverage and cannot be denied. We can suppress it, defer it, or subjugate it to someone else's "vision" of who we should be, but in the end, our desires do not dissipate.

Some individuals spend a lifetime living out someone else's "vision" of what they should do and hence live a lifetime of quiet misery. Fortunately, in other cases, individuals who start out following someone else's vision at some point reassess their lives and take a different career path. They get retrained, they indulge in hobbies related to their passions, or they make explicit changes in their career or jobs. This then puts them on a path to more contentment and, not surprisingly, greater success.

So what does this have to do with being married (or not)? Marriage is one of the few institutions or unions (much like a career pursuit) that is difficult to survive when one or more of its "players" is disingenuous about being a part of the gig (job, marriage). Irrespective of the well-meaning or sometimes downright deceitful picture individuals can paint of their dedication to the marriage cause, it is difficult for the union to survive fraudulent participation.

In that regard, marriage is one of those unique situations where at some point, the masks, and the makeovers are one way or another (gradually or forcibly) stripped away, revealing one's true self and affinity toward the union. You cannot escape the place where your heart finds true contentment.

ESSAY 10

DREAMER VERSUS CONTENTED: THE LOTTERY

TIME AND TIME again, women are often accused of having standards that are too high or unrealistic. Many women are accused of wanting something from a mate that is not practical or wanting a "perfect" person who does not exist.

There are many people who have a vision regarding their aspirations and what they want to achieve in life. They dream. And, newsflash, they work very hard to achieve their visions and dreams. At the very least, they do not "sit still" and allow a dream or vision to become unrealized simply because they did not "go after" that dream or vision.

When women have vision and they seek a companion, they often seek to join with someone who likewise dreams or is capable of envisioning something that has not yet materialized. That does not mean that these women seek someone who has already achieved everything in life, but they often at least want someone who is on the path to achievement.

Unfortunately, it is often the case that one person in the couple is dreaming, and the other person is content with their current reality. Neither party is wrong. However, a "dreamer" and a "contented" are not always a good mix. What exacerbates this is when one of the individuals has already had his or her dream manifested, and the other individual does not want to live in the existence of the realized dream. What's worse is that sometimes the "contented" wants to put breaks on the dreamer, or even more egregious, tries to have the dreamer move in reverse.

The dirty little truth in all of this is that although men and women can play either role (dreamer and contented) in a relationship, men are often unlikely to be able to coexist with a woman who has realized her dream when he has not realized his dream or he has no dream (unless *he* is the gold digger). This is manifested in a variety of scenarios. We see it in men who have difficulty in dealing with women who make more money than they do or hold a "career position" that would be superior to them in a pecking order.

In everyday living, we see men who are apartment dwellers (presumably renting and not owning) encouraging women to move out of their homes (that they have purchased) and into the men's apartments. We see it in men attempting to clip the wings of women who like to travel, encouraging women to choose to cease their leisure travel and stick closer to home. This is particularly egregious when the woman has a family (particularly adult children or grandchildren) who live elsewhere.

We also see it in subtleties, such as the answer to the question, "What would the woman do if her man won the lottery?" This question was posed to me, and to my surprise, my answer was met with a sense of indignation. I stated that if my mate won the lottery I would still work. This was not because I would not want to spend time enjoying the "spoils" that a lottery win would garner, but on the fact that I am passionate about my work, and it brings fulfillment that money cannot buy. My interpretation of the resistance I received was not based purely on the logic of working when I would not have to. It was based on the sense that no matter what the financial incentive, I still had a desire to be defined by who I am and what I contribute to society, not by what money, or a man who had money, could do for me. That was not acceptable to the man who asked me the question.

ESSAY 11

FOR THE FEMALE TWENTYSOMETHINGS

This topic was suggested by Lanta Evans Motte and Dr. Robert Brown.

TODAY'S TWENTYSOMETHING FEMALES are the beneficiaries of women and minorities who have gone before them and have fought for the equality of women. The writing of this book coincides with the first female ever in US history to be a major party's nominee for president of the United States, Hillary Clinton. Because females in their twenties have grown up with their reality being one of women in leadership being "no big deal," they have opportunities that are unparalleled by the women who have gone before them. Furthermore, based on the talent and skills today's young women possess, their potential accomplishments in life are limitless.

Many of those same women in their twenties have also grown up in a world that has largely conditioned them to believe that if they wish it, it will appear. If it doesn't appear, that is only because the "wish fairy" dropped her phone in the pedicure tub at the spa, and the phone was not soaked in rice quickly enough to save it. This same world espouses that if they lose a contest, they will still have a beautiful ribbon that signifies "A" for effort.

Unfortunately, these latter paradigms generally will not work when it comes to finding love. Finding true love is the one area of your life that cannot be manipulated, coaxed, bribed, cajoled, or forced into one's time line, or most importantly, fabricated. Hence it is perhaps one of the few things in the twentysomething's lifetime thus far on which they will have to wait to occur in its own time. Yes, one can manipulate, influence, scheme, or bribe their way into an arrangement that *mimics* true love, but the end result will be disastrous. Generations before you are plagued by individuals who have been disingenuous in their pursuit of marriage or, worse, have fallen into marriage for a myriad of not-so-constructive reasons, and through inertia have remained. Those of us who have observed these occurrences time and time again wish for a better life for you. We see that you, the twentysomethings, are beautiful young women who have accomplished a lot in the time you have lived, and are living in a time whereby life ahead is filled with the promise of greatness and extraordinary potential for happiness. Unfortunately, what we also see is that in too many instances, the example set for young women was that no accolades can compensate for the validation of being married to a man. Unfortunately, some women who are now in their thirties, forties, and beyond are realizing that being advised that they better "snag" a man quick or life is over was totally unwarranted. Some of these women are now sharing a life with someone whose biggest asset is that they too are hitched. However, for a variety of reasons, neither person is optimally happy with the life they have built together. Other women have simply succumbed to divorce.

The idea that a woman "needs" to be married in order to be validated is simply untrue. Likewise, legions of individuals have fallen for this misconception, only to live to regret the miscalculation. Furthermore, this group is larger now than at any other time in mankind's existence. (Read the introduction to this book, which references statistics on divorce and the subsequently growing singles or unmarried population.) What women of better insight wish for the twentysomething female is the patience and fortitude to go through a couple of cycles of heartache (read chapter 6: Breakups), followed by the liberating feeling that not only does life go on, life often gets *exponentially* better. Although a bout of heartache can be followed by feelings of devastation and absolute conviction that life has ended, those feelings do not have to last forever.

Moreover, the other side of that heartache is a newfound self-awareness and a keen understanding of what one needs and, most importantly, deserves.

Seasoned women have lived the cliché that "men are like buses": when one leaves the stop, another one will come along in time, without exception. Seasoned women wish for you the broadening of your perspective to see the 50 percent of women whose marriages end in divorce. (Think about what it takes to recuperate from a divorce compared to recovering from a breakup with a boyfriend.) Seasoned women wish for you the removal of your idealized view that having a man (irrespective of who he is) makes everything about life come together and flow nicely. Seasoned women do not want to see you get married and then pour your heart into raising kids the two of you have created (but only you are mainly raising), while receiving little acknowledgment from him that you are working tirelessly and sacrificing to do so. Seasoned women want you to see that if you desire to be a full-time mom, that is fantastic, and if you desire to work on a career, that is fantastic as well. But you need to know that in either case, you need a mate who is your staunchest supporter under any circumstances. Seasoned women want you to see that twenty-five, twenty-nine, thirty-five, and thirty-nine are not "ancient" ages, and that the ways in which you develop yourself between now and then will afford you the opportunities to make wiser choices in a mate, resulting in an increased chance of success in a marriage. Seasoned women want you to know that if the second happiest marital status group in American society is never-married females older than fifty (see the introduction to this book), those women know how sensational your twenties, thirties, forties, fifties, and beyond can be, irrespective of your marital status.

ESSAY 12

THE "FOOTNOTE" SPOUSE

As an older woman, never being married has revealed some interesting insights. One of the things I have realized is that I have been caught up in a sort of time vortex. My contemporaries have journeyed across a variety of family life-cycle transitions, including getting married, having children, and having grandchildren. I, on the other hand, have not experienced those transitions. However, my age has not desensitized me to those experiences, no matter how late the "seasons" of my life get. Therein lies the disconnect between me and some potential mates, which brings me to the type of scenario that has been exemplified in US history that illustrates this point.

Several years ago, former first lady, Jacqueline (Jackie) Kennedy Onassis died, and was buried at Arlington cemetery beside her first husband, President John F. Kennedy. A poignant aspect of these facts is that long after the passing of President Kennedy, Jackie remarried. However, when she was buried, the second marriage was completely overshadowed by the fact that Jackie was a former first lady.

It is not lost on me that protocol, tradition, and a host of other sociopolitical standards dictate that the one surviving spouse of a deceased US president would be buried beside that president. The fact is however, that similar scenarios are pervasive in the broader society. Chances are that a spouse will predecease the other spouse. The fact is that individuals do not give a lot of thought to the "arrangements" that should ensue when this happens. Where should the surviving spouse be buried? Should the surviving spouse be placed next to their first spouse or should arrangements be made for a resting place next to a subsequent spouse? If a marriage is a second marriage for the man or woman and they live in a home that was previously occupied by one of the spouses and their original spouse, what happens to the home when the original owner passes? Should people be buried on the soil on which they grew up, if they have moved away and married someone?

These questions are for me the foundations of what I call the "footnote" spouse. A footnote spouse is someone who is not afforded the totality of consideration of a spouse as the main, first, or "alpha" spouse. The Jackie Kennedy scenario reminds me of some experiences I have had with *some* men who have been married and particularly have had children. There is a "been there, done that" approach to building a post-divorce relationship with a different mate. These divorcés operate as if their previous marriages and family units are the ones that really count and, therefore, the only ones that will truly matter. Every relationship subsequent to that marriage is an epilogue, a "footnote." For them, the core story has been told and has ended. (I do not necessarily think they do this on a conscious level.)

I am not intending to be the "footnote" to someone's life. A footnote is placed at the bottom of a page. It is far from being a "leading character" in the text. It is an auxiliary tool used to support the main theme. In that regard, I understand the realities of the fierce dedication to the memory of a former spouse, and the children born of that union. However, men and women need to understand that the composition of a family becomes irrevocably changed as a result of death or divorce.

If I become involved with someone who is divorced or has survived a spouse, I want to be *integrated* into the new reality of the family structure, and I am willing to do my part to do what is needed to work on that new configuration. I understand that when someone is divorced, their former spouse and children are not going anywhere (nor do I need or want them to). However, the story of the lives involved becomes transformed for everyone when there is a divorce. The principals' roles become altered and reconfigured. Too many people want to treat divorce as if they were remodeling a house to add a bathroom, but they try to stick the bathroom randomly to an exterior wall of the house, when a more practical design would involve the reconfiguration of the interior of the home. I can only say that for me, and the house in which I reside, footnotes will be used exclusively for writing, not for functioning in a relationship. (Note: Not all second marriages have a "footnote" tone. Nancy and Ronald Regan certainly did not.)

PART 2

DATING AND COMPATIBILITY

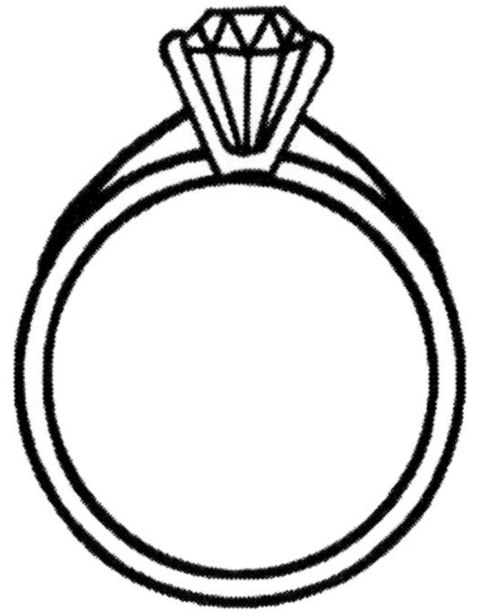

ESSAY 13

PERFECT FOR ME

Mr./Ms. Right	Mr./Ms. Perfect
Mr./Ms. Right Now	Mr./Ms. Perfect for Me

A TREMENDOUS PET peeve for many never-married individuals is always being accused of looking for someone who is perfect. Admittedly, there are those among us (and among you, I might add) who fit that description, but by and large, perfection is not our end game. Let me delineate some things that I seek that would not fall under the category of "perfection."

Someone who

- has some level of spirituality;
- has respect for mankind;
- has some moral fiber;
- has compatible life goals both individually and together;
- has shared values;
- has the X factor (chemistry) with me;
- appropriately prioritizes the relationship;
- desires a monogamous relationship;
- respects my life choices and I respect theirs;
- seeks optimal communication;
- has demonstrated a history of providing financial support for themselves (or evidence of time well spent on identifying options for legitimate financial viability);
- has some shared recreational interests;

- has the ability to settle down;
- does not abuse alcohol or drugs (I would consider negotiating working through counseling or rehabilitation for either of these.); and
- does not engage in illegal activity.

I think it would be fair to say that lacking any one of the above qualities has been the cornerstone of innumerable counseling sessions with relationship coaches and counselors for many couples. Yet when single individuals "pass" on individuals after numerous rounds of struggling to achieve harmony on any of the above, we are labeled as wanting a "perfect" relationship.

Perhaps if those who dive into marriage before rectifying these issues would follow our lead, there would be fewer divorces.

ESSAY 14

I NEED TO BE AN EQUAL PARTNER, NOT A PROTEGE

A FEW YEARS ago, I was having a conversation with one of my well-respected professional mentors who is a married male older than sixty. He has two professional adult daughters. One is a physician and the other one practices law. My mentor and I were discussing the challenges that professional women of my generation have with regard to connecting with a mate. The dialogue we were having was the continuation of many discussions that he, his wife, and I have had previously on the subject. During this particular conversation, my mentor expressed a revelation he had just had regarding my position on the subject. He exclaimed, "You're looking for a partner!"

What was intriguing about his statement was that the concept of a woman being a "partner" in a relationship had not previously been a part of his perspective on the male-female paradigm. This "partnership" perspective was a foreign issue for him. At the time, he embodied for me the arc of distortion that is present in most of my contemporaries' efforts to build relationships with potential mates.

Our society operates within a paradigm that says men are providers and thus the leaders of their households. I do not espouse that male household leadership in its purest form is problematic. What has become an issue is that this leadership has manifested in the notion that wives (significant others) are subordinate to their husbands in every manner imaginable.

I do not have a problem with a male being the "head" (leader) of a household. (Some women might have a problem with that, and that is their right.) I have a problem with the fact that this male-dominated leadership manifests itself in the assumption that my role is that of an eternal protégé; that I need guidance and direction from a husband. I had problems with this notion even when I was in my twenties. Certainly now that I am in my fifties and have amassed volumes of experience, wisdom, knowledge, and "survival skills," it is unconscionable to think that I somehow now "need" someone to guide me and direct my path. What I want is to join forces with someone who understands that what I bring to a relationship, combined with what my mate brings to a relationship, establishes a whole that is greater than the sum of its parts. When two souls can truly "leverage" their respective attributes, the resulting whole yields maximum strength.

ESSAY 15

TOGETHERNESS

This essay was inspired by Pamela Cheryl Higgins Harris.

My likes and desires can present a bit of a paradox. On the one hand, I live a very full and dynamic life (combining career, service, family, and social activities). On the other hand, I thrive on consistent and authentic companionship. I am attracted to men who live similarly dynamic lives. Two people who have very "full" lives do not have exceptional amounts of time to spend with each other. Therefore, some strategy and negotiation need to take place between those two people for a relationship between them to peacefully (and lovingly) coexist. That requires some honest and realistic consideration. For one, I have to understand that if I am joined with a dynamic individual, he will more often than not have activities that will not include me, thus impeding on *our* time together. Therefore, we'd have to work together to ensure that we are spending a mutually acceptable amount of time together that is healthy for the relationship. However, we'd both also need to be willing to make reasonable sacrifices with respect to our "outside" activities in order to honor the priority of our union. Hence, if I am involved with someone who has a life that requires him to be heavily engaged in activities that don't involve me, I'd need to be a priority for his free time, and of course I'd owe him the same courtesy.

I often think that if I am supposedly in a relationship with someone but we spend minimal time together, what is the benefit of being in that relationship? By the same token, if he does not engage in activities with me that I deem really fun (or is unwilling to make a "sacrifice" on occasion to do so), again I ask, what is the benefit of the relationship? In my view, what would be missing is the "togetherness," an essential aspect of being in a relationship.

Therein lies the rub. When two people are leading separate lives and essentially are just sharing living quarters, this for me is not togetherness because they are not sharing their time with each other. In actuality, their individual free time is spent doing the things apart that do not necessarily incorporate their mates. Examples include hanging out with the fellas (or girls), or even being home but being antisocial and not interacting with their mates.

When I think about my experiences as well as the ways in which I have lived vicariously through others, I recognize that the concept of "togetherness" in a relationship has been a source of contention. "Togetherness" on the one hand seems intuitive and straightforward. However, when its existence is dissected in a relationship, it is not uncommon to find that rather than being straightforward, it has a multitude of meanings, and invariably it is different for everyone or at least changes over the course of people's relationships.

I submit that when we think about the "glue" of relationships, the question of how a couple spends time together becomes a sticking point (pun perhaps intended). "Togetherness" has multiple dimensions that are exhibited through a variety of questions. How much time does a couple spend together? What are they doing when they spend that time together? What is an acceptable formula for the amount of time spent with people outside of the couple or with people just being by themselves when they are in a relationship? What is an acceptable amount of time a couple spends with individuals outside of the marriage (on a social basis) compared to the time spent with their mate? How does the enjoyment felt when time is spent with people outside of the marriage compare to the enjoyment felt with time spent with one's mate? Does the relationship appear *obvious* to everyone around? (Are the nonverbals of a relationship [touching, hugging, kissing, admiring glances] readily apparent?) What is a reasonable level of negotiation on these issues?

Of course every couple has the right to define these issues in a way that is mutually agreeable to them. Although their formula might not work for all other couples, it *must* work for the two people who are in the relationship.

It occurred to me that this issue was a consideration for me when I was in my early twenties. I recall attending a party with some girlfriends when we noticed the arrival of a couple. At our age, seeing couples at a party was a bit of an anomaly. The thing that struck my girlfriends and me about this couple, and thus the basis for my remembering the scenario, was that the guy was deliberate in introducing his date to a number of friends at the party. It was noticeably apparent that the guy was the one in the couple that was familiar with the attendees at the party. However, it was obvious that he was on a date and he was proud to be with her. The striking and memorable part was that shortly after their arrival, he took the time to escort her around the room and introduce her to his friends. Again, at twentysomething, this behavior was not typical of my male contemporaries. (Truthfully, not much of this behavior had been demonstrated throughout my thirties, forties, and fifties.) People in general attended parties stag (without a date). And, if they did bring dates, you could not always tell by the body language of the couple that they were on a date.

Although this could be interpreted as benign or a nonissue, I believe the symbolism is quite poignant. Many couples seem to exist as independent people who share a space, as opposed to united people who have come together to share a life. These separate lives are exhibited through the fact that they either do not spend a lot of time together, or when they do spend time together, their interaction is limited, of low quality, or does not read "couple."

ESSAY 16

WHY NOT ROUND UP ALL THE "GOOD PEOPLE"?

THERE ARE MULTITUDES of great people in this world. Although greatness might very well be subject to interpretation, at a basic level it is not too difficult to find people who generally are good human beings. The downside of all this positivity when it comes to matchmaking is that people often view raw goodness in one person as being a universal fit for basic companionship with almost anybody else.

It is funny how many human beings hold this view when they wholeheartedly directly and indirectly acknowledge that it is a concept that is nonconducive to any other arena. We would not generally want to crossbreed two different types of animals because they are both gentle souls and would make good house pets. We would not suggest that a Bentley and a Mercedes-Maybach interchange auto parts and make a new version of luxury.

Yet matchmakers will become acquainted with two different "good" or "nice" individuals and decide that the two of them should be together. The myth surrounding never-married people is that they are not acquainted with good people or have not been involved with good people.

Never-married people recognize that although "goodness" might be an excellent *baseline* for building a meaningful relationship or friendship, it is not the one-dimensional characteristic on which one can unequivocally build an excellent romantic relationship. The relationship (lifelong mate) dynamic is a detailed and often complicated one. Goodness of character is but one aspect of what makes someone a good mate. Although the absence of goodness might very well be a deal breaker, the presence of goodness does not necessarily create a deal maker. There are infinite combinations of characteristics, personal qualities, personalities, backgrounds, interests, life goals, and so on, that create a solid platform for a good romantic relationship. Admittedly, for those individuals who have used the "insert spouse here" strategy for marriage, "goodness" might very well have been the sole attribute taken into consideration. For more seasoned singles, that singular approach is generally not enough.

ESSAY 17

SOMEONE ELSE'S AGENDA

In immeasurable instances throughout many people's lives there have been a cadre of individuals who believe they have the divine right to make life-mate choices for *other* people. Those often well-intentioned busybodies think they should have a hand in determining who is right for you. Often they are invested in someone else's life choice to the point where no protestation from the person whose life is at stake is ever heard or understood. How many of you know of at least one instance when someone knew leading up to their wedding day that they were flat out making a mistake, only to have one of their "handlers" determine that come hell or high water they were going to go through with the marriage? I am not speaking of the "shotgun marriage" scenario (whereby a pregnancy has occurred and the father [baby daddy] is forced to do the honorable thing). I speak of general instances whereby at some point people realize that the person with whom they are involved is simply not the person with whom they want to spend the rest of their lives.

There is a lot to be said for wisdom in general. Wisdom does not cease because the subject of relationships or marriage is on the table. However, wisdom does not trump one's gut for what is right for them. Other people simply cannot be the primary determinants of what is right for us. The decision of who a life mate should be is a decision that needs to be wholeheartedly felt between the two individuals who are the actual individuals joining together.

Too often, other kinds of agendas enter into a couple's decision to marry. Those agendas include economics, class status, pregnancy, and even plain old "saving face" on the wedding day because pulling the plug is simply too embarrassing. Woeful statistics on marriage and gut-wrenching stories of the misery people experience when they have not made the choice for themselves challenge the notion that someone else's agenda will sustain a marriage.

ESSAY 18

MARRIAGE IS NOT A GROUP PROJECT

Let's get this straight...basically 50 percent of marriages in the United States end in divorce. More than 60 percent of second marriages end in divorce, and more than 70 percent of third marriages end in divorce. (Refer to the introduction of this book.) Why then, when someone has the courage, fortitude, foresight, wisdom, presence of mind, independent thinking, strength, or "audacity" to pull the plug on a relationship (at any stage), is there still a chorus of individuals who want them to "stay the course"?

Are we so conditioned by the "norm" to be mated or married that when someone tells us that the condition just is not optimal for them at that time, we just cannot accept that someone is "just saying no"? How is it that we have become so desensitized to people's feelings that we nearly force individuals into a status that they themselves do not feel is right for them?

How many times have we heard these words: "I knew from the beginning that it just did not feel right. I wanted to call the wedding off, but my family, friends, and so forth, just would not let me. My loved ones did not want to be embarrassed by my not going through with the wedding ceremony." Do we harbor a "misery loves company" feeling when we are witnessing the potential union of two people? Do we provide advice that is in the best interest of the people to whom we are providing the advice or to ourselves?

One of the most common reasons for being encouraged to stay in a relationship is that everyone is not perfect. Although truer words could not be said, the lack of perfection is but a fraction of the reasons why some people wish to discontinue a relationship. I have never heard any person say they are looking for a perfect person. I think it is only fair that they seek the person who is perfect for them. (Refer to essay 13: "Perfect for Me.") However, those outside the union between two people often insist on inserting themselves as the key relationship decision makers. How many times have individuals taken the walk down the aisle with the feeling that the person at the altar *is* the perfect one for them, only to participate in the divorce process later? Is it not then reasonable that the person who has a more pragmatic view of a mate should be left alone when he or she dares to act on that pragmatism, thus terminating a relationship?

There is major hypocrisy in the fact that never-married individuals are often chastised for rendering advice to their married friends about their marriages. However, the divorced, separated, or otherwise miserably married people can push someone toward marriage and that is OK. It is time we all recalibrate our instincts and realize that the decision to get married is not a group project.

E S S A Y 1 9

SELF-IMPOSED GLASS CEILING

Women have particularly been victimized by the "glass ceiling" concept at work. This is a term used to describe a culture in many work environments whereby women are not seen to be capable of handling responsibilities beyond a certain plateau in an organization. Part of this culture includes the fact that many men cannot see themselves having to report to a woman who is a superior. Furthermore, many men in organizations cannot see a woman being the absolute "head" of an organization.

Women also run into a glass ceiling of sorts in their dating lives. Sometimes the glass ceiling is one that is attempted to be imposed on them. Sometimes the glass ceiling is one that their potential mates impose on themselves.

The way women experience glass ceilings in their relationships is that their mates are discouraging and sometimes downright rude and disrespectful toward women whenever those women endeavor to reach beyond a capacity they have already attained. Examples are when a woman's husband does not want to see her expand her education or pursue a career that would bring with it an increased level of self-respect and, above all, *money*. When women are facing the relationship glass ceiling, their mates might go as far as to belittle them in their efforts to improve their overall conditions.

Conversely, many men have set hierarchical limits on themselves. In that regard, they are content with having reached a moderate level of achievement and do not wish to go any further. (Please note that I think people have every right to determine for themselves what it is in life they wish to achieve.) What is most important is that every adult is self-sustaining, does no harm to others, and provides service to mankind whenever, wherever, and at whatever level is practical for them.

The problem is that if two people have materially different visions of their respective plateaus, peaceful coexistence is often difficult at best. This fact would not be much of an issue if it were not for a culture that is patriarchal and, therefore, does not deal well when the "female" is the one who has the lofty ambition and subsequent accomplishments. As previously mentioned, two people who are not like-minded in ambition can make for a relationship that is problematic. When it is the woman who has the noticeable ambition, it is difficult for her to be with someone who does not share the same level of ambition.

Women are often accused of not broadening their spectrum on whom they date. On the contrary, there are infinite examples of women who have tried to assist men who have said they want to raise the bar on their expectations of themselves. However, at times when these two get together, the women are soon met with resistance because sometimes these men have a self-imposed glass ceiling. Furthermore, there are instances when these men then attempt to move their self-imposed glass ceiling over to their mates. Although this mismatch can work on occasion, it is often difficult for people on divergent trajectories to *thrive* in a relationship.

ESSAY 20

ONLINE DATING: #PATIENCE AND PRAGMATISM

I HAVE EXPERIENCED online dating. That is not because I have had a problem *meeting* men in general. The issue for me is finding that "special" person. That said, contrary to some stereotypes, an Internet dating site is not a place inhabited exclusively by the misfits and ne'er-do-wells of society. As a matter of fact, I have come across the profiles of a few men I have known previously throughout the years from a variety of other affiliations, and trust me, these particular men are the polar opposite of misfit. As a matter of fact, they are of good character, exceptionally well accomplished, *and* easy on the eyes. In addition, a number of the new men whom I have met because of these sites have been fantastic individuals. However, there are some things to be considered when using these sites.

Although these sites help make our dating activities more efficient, patience is key. My unscientific calculation is that on one particular site, before I actually planned a date with someone from the site, I read in excess of fifty profiles, identified five men with whom I wished to exchange phone numbers, and of those five men, went on a date with one of them. From my point of view, investing some leisure time in going through profiles and ultimately having a date is efficient compared to the preparations needed to leave my house countless times for a variety of activities whereby I "might" meet someone of interest.

Pragmatism and thick skin are also key when being on a dating site. Not unlike conventional interactions that take place during the course of our lives, on a dating site, there are going to be individuals with whom you are attracted but the feeling is not mutual. A dating site is not a "genie in a bottle." The rich executive bachelor might be on the site (for a minute); however, he is not spending countless hours seeking an introverted woman who does not want to post her picture or do much to describe herself on the site.

Most importantly, your gut, intuition, and instincts are to be keenly respected. You can generally discern key clues regarding someone's character through a combination of reading their profiles, looking at the pictures they have *chosen* to post, communicating with them in writing via the site, and listening to them on the phone. If your gut sends red flags about someone at any point, you should absolutely listen to that intuition. If you don't feel there has been enough information provided in someone's profile for *your* comfort level in making a reasonably informed decision about that individual, then go with your gut.

During the initial phases of becoming acquainted with someone you have met online, you should treat them as a stranger because, guess what? They are! Irrespective of what they say or how comfortable you may feel, *never* invite them to your house for an initial date and *never* go to their home for an initial date. Always have an initial face-to-face meeting in a neutral, public place that is well lit and well patronized. A location in a popular mall is a great place. And always phone a relative or friend (preferably someone in close geographic proximity to the date location) to tell them you are having a first date with someone you met online. Give that relative or friend the name and phone number of the person you are meeting. Also, have a specific time when you are expecting to be with your date for that relative or friend to phone you. Receiving a well-timed phone call during the date signals to your date that someone cares about you and that if something is wrong, the person who cares about you will know it rather quickly and will take action immediately to determine if there is a problem.

I would characterize dating sites as the cyber versions of our dating experiences offline. On occasion, we click with someone we meet (pun perhaps intended); however, we are not guaranteed to find the "one" in three quick keystrokes. (Note: In case you are considering giving this a try, *Good Morning America* once reported that the first couple of weeks after Christmas is a peak time for activity on Internet dating sites.)

ESSAY 21

SEX–THE QUESTION ON EVERYONE'S MIND

THE SIX-MILLION-DOLLAR QUESTION is whether we are getting any [sex]. The fifty-cent answer is we don't kiss and tell. However, I will address the subject.

Sex is a physiological need. In plain English, this means that some scholars (e.g., Abraham Maslow) purport that sex is as essential to human beings as are food and water. However, the activity of engaging in sexual behavior has become one of the key ways of determining a *woman's* reputation. That determination is largely based on religious and spiritual beliefs. Therein lies tremendous cultural or societal conflict.

I have the utmost respect for religious dogma when it comes to the concept of realizing that engaging in sexual activity is intended to be exclusive to a man and a woman who have made a commitment to marriage before God. However, the conflict derived from what sex is to the human body versus what it represents from a religious perspective has caused countless examples of extreme behavior in our society.

Elizabeth Taylor is representative of one of those extremes. A key reason she had so many husbands is not because she suffered from "serial marriage syndrome." Her marriages were largely a response to her desire to keep her reputation as a "lady" intact. She (not unlike most of us) had natural urges regarding sex, and she kept herself "honest" by marrying many of the men who were the objects of those urges. Taylor's background was characterized by a rather puritanical upbringing and beliefs, which led her to live a life that reflected the notion that love was synonymous with marriage.[1] This in hindsight prevented her from being perceived as someone who "slept around."

A woman I knew who was happily married with three young daughters represented another of those extremes. When her oldest daughter was elementary school age, the woman proclaimed she wanted to see her daughter get married at age seventeen. This wish was also based on her desire to preserve her daughter's "reputation." The woman's strategy was that her daughter could get married. The daughter and her new husband could then live with the woman and her husband and enjoy a nice lifestyle while being newly married and pursuing their respective college careers. Most of all, the purity of her daughter's reputation could remain intact. Problem solved?

By most people's standards, both of these examples are lifestyle extremes brought forth based on the sole purpose of preserving a woman's purity and reputation.

Perspectives on sex or marriage are as diverse among older, never-married individuals as the diversity of thought on the subject is in any other group. However, one thing that I would submit, which is largely a shared philosophy among us fifty-plus folks, is that we have not allowed the need for sexual intimacy to trump an otherwise reasonable evaluation of whether or not to marry.

As in most other aspects of our lives, we manage our sexual activities in a practical manner, recognizing the societal or religious norms while balancing the reality of physiological needs. Common sense also plays a role in our considerations.

---

1 Richard Meryman, "I Refuse to Cure My Public Image," *Life*, December 18, 1964, 74, https://books.google.fi/books?id=kFEEAAAAMBAJ&lpg=PP1&ots=xZJGAWxygn&pg=PA74&redir_esc=y#v=onepage&q&f=false.

PART 3

TRUTH BE TOLD

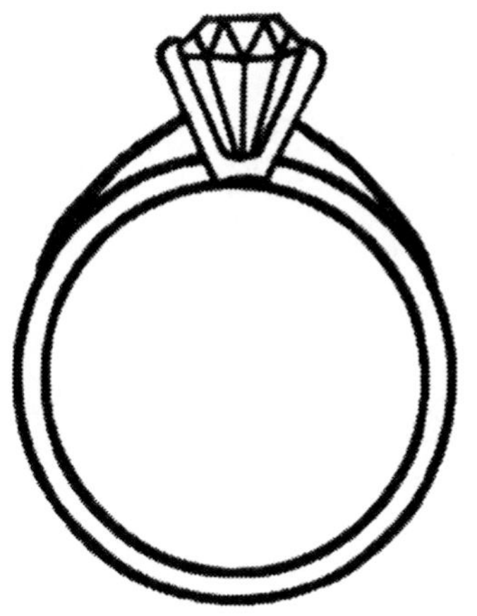

ESSAY 22

WHY IS THE WOMAN OFTEN CONSIDERED THE PROBLEM?

Many of the writings in popular culture that address male-female relationships focus on what the woman is or is not doing. It seems that many authors always seem to identify the woman as being at the core of relationship issues. I will acquiesce that women are largely the gender that are the most vocal and active in the dialogue of how to find a mate.

Ironically, there are volumes of literature on men that are not particularly flattering. Men are often painted as immature (at the very least, less mature than their female counterparts until well into their twenties). Men are also often said to not be naturally monogamous, not necessarily smarter than women, at times overly aggressive, and not particularly organized or neat.

Yet when the issue of dating dilemmas is raised, it is the woman who suddenly is the bearer of most of the problems. This is quite perplexing to me.

I will admit that one does not have to go far to find hordes of women who spend an inordinate amount of time obsessing over when, where, and how they will find a great man. Beyond having the obsession, they consume much of their lives invoking tactics for "snagging" a man. Sometimes these tactics go beyond the ethical.

I tire of hearing that women need to try doing one thing or another if they want to find a man. It seems to me that if you have a species (men) who by nature or nurture have to be continuously guided toward "settling down," and you have "love-starved" women who seek a "ready-made" husband who wants to settle down, what you really have is a perfect storm that continuously erupts in all the ways a storm can wreak havoc on an existence (e.g., ill-conceived marriages, divorce, unplanned pregnancies, and overall misery).

Can we just stop pointing fingers and deal with reality? With the preponderance of the aforementioned, it's a wonder any "person" of decent character can find a mate in the village of the whacky. Can we just pull the plug on the foolishness, get back to being decent and aboveboard, and let love reign?

ESSAY 23

THE "GOOD CATCH"-MATRIMONY AS REHABILITATION

THERE ARE THOSE men and women who have gone through most of their lives not being held to standards that instill in them the necessity of taking responsibility for their own actions. Some of these individuals were the toddlers who never had age-appropriate boundaries set for them. They grew into children whose wayward actions were defended by a guardian's chant, "He is just being a child. All children go through some things." These same kids might have become adolescents whose negative behavior might have become increasingly more serious with actions that were increasingly more egregious. Yet again, a guardian's refrain might get elevated to, "He's hanging around the wrong crowd." Still, these individuals are generally not routinely tasked with accepting responsibilities (and consequences) for their own actions.

This child eventually becomes an adult, and guess what? The guardian now wants to hand him or her over to someone who will continue to enable the behavior or, even better (or worse), become a part of a rehabilitation strategy. At this point, a "good catch" must be found because if a "bad crowd" was the former reason for ill behavior, certainly a "good catch" will be the remedy for him or her to function as a productive citizen.

Hence therein lies the strategy from the parents, guardians, or loved ones to search for a "mate" for the wayward ward. The union between the ward and this "savior" of a person is probably a recipe for yet another failed marriage. How often do we hear that a man needs a good woman in his life to make him the great person that he can be (irrespective of the lack of evidence heretofore)? Although *sometimes* a "good mate" is the answer, other times, *it simply is not.*

All too often, individuals who appear to be "good catches" are targeted to be the matrimonial rehabilitators of individuals who otherwise have limited evidence of having their lives together. People who have enabled bad behavior in their wards appear to actively recruit a good person to help rectify the lives of the wards, who have not demonstrated that they can live a mischief-free life. The "good catch" is targeted as someone who can make life all better for the wayward ward.

Aside from the inherent flaw in that strategy, what does that say about the expectation that people who have tried to "live right" should somehow "sacrifice" to devote their lives to the rehabilitation of someone who, for whatever reason, does not have it together? If the case is that the "opposite attracting" souls come together of their own accord and find "perfection" in each other, then bravo! However, if the union is contrived from a strategy to recruit a positive influence for someone, then that is quite unfortunate. People should not be made to feel that they have any less right than anyone else to seek someone with whom they are "equally yoked." Two souls coming together, on their own terms, and making each other better is fantastic. One soul who becomes a better person because they have optimally leveraged the benefit of being "mated" in a way that is uplifting for both parties is also great. However, saddling one person as a remedy for another person's problems is not OK.

ESSAY 24

SELF-MAINTENANCE VERSUS HIGH-MAINTENANCE

Eldridge R. (Roddy) Allen and Solomon Irwin Royster provided the title and concept for this essay.

NEEDLESS TO SAY, by now you can glean that there are countless realities that lead to being older, never married, *and* happy! There are two questions that are sometimes asked of me with respect to my happiness. One is, "How on earth can you be happy?" The other is, "What kind of standards do you have for the man you seek?" These questions (on occasion) allude to common myths in our society. One obvious myth is that a woman cannot possibly be fulfilled unless she has "Mrs." in front of her name. Another myth is that if she is not married by the time she is past her twenties, she must be high maintenance. The fact is that many of us are the exact opposite of high maintenance. We are self-maintained.

What does this mean? An older woman who has never been married and is happy has most likely filled her life with activities that make her content, and activities that have allowed her to fully develop who she is. For me, the first half century of my life was filled with spending quality time with friends and family, pursuing higher education (all the way through to a doctoral degree), and having two different but related careers. The first career was in marketing and sales in a major corporation. The second career is as a marketing professor. In addition, I have traveled fairly extensively throughout the United States and have traveled abroad. I have also vacationed on one of the largest cruise ships in the world. As for other "fun," I thoroughly enjoy the "usual" activities, such as attending concerts and plays, going to the movies, going to live sporting events, and visiting amusement parks. Because I thoroughly enjoy dancing, I have spent the last several years taking line dance classes, and more recently Zumba classes. In my life's activities, I have invested in me. I have explored life's offerings on my own terms, satisfying my appetite for developing myself while also responding to the curiosity I have had about life in general. Hence I have not looked to someone else to make me happy. The ironic truth of the matter is that arguably, many of the women who have *not* done a lot for themselves are the ones who can be high maintenance because they *need* someone else to provide "things" that will make them happy or maintain a lifestyle or persona that they believe they deserve (but have rarely earned for themselves).

Rest assured, my being self-maintained is not to be confused with not wanting or needing a mate. (See essay 3: "A Woman's Best Accessory?") Our society has confused a woman's ability to provide for herself with her not wanting a mate. If "provision" were the key criterion for my choice in selecting a mate, I would have surrendered myself to the highest bidder a long time ago. I dare say a union based largely on material gain is a troubled union that quite possibly suffers an untimely demise.

The difference between many who have gotten married and me is that I have always been honest with myself regarding whether a particular romantic interest is truly an optimal *lifetime* fit. That involves evaluating characteristics that go far beyond just being able to provide. Spirituality, integrity, a spirit of generosity, and good old common sense top the list of qualities that are important to me. Monetary status in anyone's life can change at any time. Above all, timing and destiny are key factors in finding the right mate.

To the ill-informed, I might appear to be high maintenance. I *want* a man in my life to partner with me, recognizing that I am a person who is constantly striving to be a better me. (See essay 14: "I Need to Be a Partner, Not a Protégé.") I do not need a man for the purpose of taking care of me or completing me. Hence the man of my dreams can continue to live his life in a way that is fulfilling to him, while we each benefit from our unwavering support of each other's goals. He will not be required to continually respond to my infinite *need* for "something," which would be the case if I were high maintenance. (Side note: Cards, flowers, and gifts are always welcome!)

ESSAY 25

QUALITY VERSUS QUANTITY: CAREERS AND MARRIAGES

ONE OF THE much-used clichés in our society is the concept of quality versus quantity. "Quality time" is often the default justification of someone who is accused of not spending enough time with someone. The quality time concept suggests that devotion to someone should be evaluated on the quality of the interactions that occur between two people. The underlying philosophy is that the quantity of time spent together is of less importance.

Relationships struggle with this conundrum. It seems that for many couples, there is simply not enough time spent together, particularly for recreation, vacation, or just plain old fun. It is not unusual for relationships or marriages to be subordinated to careers. Although there is an overwhelming practical aspect to this reality (income is needed to support our lifestyles), and marriages often suffer because of it.

I have had careers in private industry as well as in higher education. I have observed the level of time, energy, and dedication many people are willing to devote to a career. What's interesting is that that same level of commitment is absent from many relationships.

Most career professionals who are my contemporaries, and whom I have observed through the years, have been adamant about the time and energy they must put into their jobs. Long hours during weekdays, weekend hours, and holidays are all often dominated by work. Many of these professionals would find it simply inexcusable to not be present and in the moment for all the specifics and details that go along with the day-to-day activities associated with their jobs. For these professionals, quality cannot compensate for quantity.

Conversely, some of these same professionals who are married will relegate their relationships to the philosophy that quality time is good enough. Hence at their jobs almost everything is a priority and virtually nothing is left unattended. Conversely at home, quality time is all that is needed, often leaving people and things unattended. At an extreme level, if quality time at home cannot be provided, then the default is that the mate or family should be grateful for simply being afforded the great lifestyle to which they have become accustomed as a result of the professional's long hours at work.

I am well aware that many people's careers demand extraordinary levels of devotion that require hours that go above and beyond a standard work week. However, I think it rather ironic that for many of them, the people in their lives are afforded a fraction of that devotion. A significant other's important occasions and milestones often get rationed attention that is justified as quality time. Yet job commitments are almost always given the respect of quantity as a foundation for quality. Perhaps that might be why some people's careers are far more successful than their married lives.

ESSAY 26

POSTPONEMENT

In my younger years, I would make a practice of accumulating "things," being mindful of creating a comfortable life for myself. For example, although like many young professionals I was an apartment dweller, when I bought furniture I "invested" in that furniture. In spite of the fact that I could not afford extremely expensive furniture pieces, I would still procure quality pieces that I could envision in my future house. I recall quite vividly that some took another approach. They would buy furniture that was close to disposable instead, opting to wait to buy the "nice stuff" when they would someday buy a house. My thought was that when I buy a house, I might very well not be able to afford "good" furniture to put in it. Besides, I wanted to enjoy the present and not postpone my indulgence of "nice" things for the future.

That philosophy toward buying furniture was symbolic of my approach to life in general. Although I knew I wanted to someday marry, I was not going to deny myself the pleasures of life while on the quest for matrimony. As such, I purchased a house, occasionally took vacations, and accumulated a nice asset or two along the way.

Some view these practices as a statement of fierce independence and a form of "declaration" regarding my entrenchment in my single status. I say these assumptions are the product of closed minds and narrow, antiquated thinking. I have simply been truly living my life and indulging in activities that truly make me happy!

ESSAY 27

THAT "COUGAR" THING

OUR SOCIETY HAS no shortage of double standards when it comes to acceptable behavior for men compared to women. The subject of relationships is not immune to those contradictions. One of the relationship-pairing scenarios that often raises eyebrows is when there is a substantive age difference between the two people. However, a woman who is the one in the couple that is more "senior" is often targeted with more than just a raised eyebrow. Admittedly, I think it is safe to say that the older the couple is, the more tolerant society becomes in general with significant age differences within a couple.

Although men who date or marry women who are significantly younger might get double takes or side eyes when they are in public, this May-December romance (older man, younger woman) is often better accepted than the romance between an older woman and a younger man.

Older women with younger men have been labeled "cougars." This moniker is meant to denote that somehow the older woman has hunted down and captured her relatively helpless prey for her own satisfaction. Although older men *and* women who have relationships with younger mates might be labeled "cradle robbers," society has not labeled men with a term that suggests that they have preyed on younger women, like the "cougar" term. Conversely, the young woman is often labeled as being after the man's money, or having some other motivation that is equally disingenuous. Hence, irrespective of which end of the age-spectrum the woman is on in the relationship, she is still more than likely cast as the villain in the relationship.

One can find examples of older men *and* older women who have sought companionship with significantly younger individuals for less than honorable intentions. However, women are almost always ascribed some aspect of negativity when they are the older person in the pairing. This fact flies in the face of the backdrop of the male-dominated culture in which we live. Why is it that there are infinite examples of women needing to gain their rightful place in a variety of aspects of their lives—marriage, career, purchasing power—yet when they are the significantly older person in a couple, suddenly these women are perceived to have detrimentally dominant power?

The fact remains that men (boys) are largely socialized practically from the womb to behave as if they are in control of the society, and they are the dominant gender. From a relationship standpoint, this often manifests itself in that men are generally the ones who "go after" the women they want in their lives. Why is it that when a man is the significantly younger person in a relationship, it is assumed that he was no longer that dominant force?

There are infinite examples of men who exercise their dominance over women irrespective of the women's age. We see it when men refer to women as "girls," even when the women are significantly older than they are, and the women perhaps have a career-oriented ranking over them. We see it when young men refer to their divorced fathers' love interests as "girls." These are their fathers' age-appropriate companions who could one day be their stepmothers. In other words, these women who are old enough to be these boys' mothers and warrant respect are being referred to as "girls," as if they are in high school.

Couples that are characterized by an older woman and a younger man often have a dynamic that is commensurate with the socialization of men in society overall. That is, the man pursued the woman, and the man feels he has the characteristics (e.g., birth right, superiority, finances, power, and drive) that make him her equal, if not her superior.

The essay, "Loving Your Child, Disrespecting Me" (essay 38), alludes to our culture as one whereby children are sometimes afforded the status of an adult. This is especially the case with male children who experience their parents' divorce. Little boys are sometimes called "men" before they are old enough to know how to spell the word "boy" or "man." Young boys and teens are often referred to as "men" by other adult men. Why then should we think that young men perceive boundaries when it comes to going after older women? Whenever we want to label an older woman with a younger man as a "cougar," we need to be more introspective about how we socialize our boys!

There are countless young men who pursue older women for relationships for a variety of reasons. Some do so because they generally view older women as the people with whom they feel the greatest kinship. Some people in general are "old souls."

ESSAY 28

DEAR MARRIED WOMEN, I AM NOT YOUR ENEMY

The unfortunate truth in our society is that too many individuals violate the sacred trust that is the union between two married individuals. This trust can be violated by one or both of the individuals in the union or someone outside of the union.

Single individuals are often the presumed "culprits" of the infidelity that plagues some marriages. Single women in particular are often targeted by married women as potential sources of their husbands' indiscretions. Although single women (and men for that matter) are sometimes guilty of these improprieties, not all single people are culprits.

As I have stated a number of times in this book, I have wanted to be married since I can remember. That remains so as an adult. The other fact of the matter is that I have not given up on the desire to marry someone who is wholeheartedly devoted to me (and I to him). *This required level of devotion by default excludes married men.*

I wish for some married women that they would cease to look on single women as vixens on the hunt for any man they can find. For many older individuals who never married, we have been discriminating in our search for a mate all our lives. That selectivity does not cease to exist when we come across a married woman's husband. As a matter of fact, he is the antithesis of what we are looking for because he is married; therefore, he is not the prime candidate for providing us with the love and devotion we require and are yearning to reciprocate.

If we run across a married man who seems all too willing to indulge us in an inappropriate way, he further demonstrates how much he is not the man we seek. He is showing us one of the myriad reasons why we have not yet taken the plunge, and furthermore why he has excluded himself from our consideration as a candidate for marriage.

I'll say something else to married women: the individuals you *really* need to keep your eye on are some of your married female friends (and frenemies). Unlike many of us never-married females, some of these married women are miserable because they consider themselves "stuck" with spouses they no longer love. When they come across a married man, they see in him someone with whom they could possibly share a kinship; someone who might possibly be discontented in *his* marriage, and someone with whom they can share similar risk levels for cheating. One final note: if your husband is cheating on you or has a wandering eye, that is inexcusable on countless levels, and you have my sympathies. However, the fact of the matter is that *he* is the individual who has made a commitment to you. Stop directing your venom at other women and target the culprit who deserves your wrath: *your* husband!

ESSAY 29

SEX AS A CHORE?

Some people are totally aghast at the notion that sex can be considered a chore. Well now, let's look at this phenomenon. First and foremost, there are varying comfort levels among individuals when it comes to being sexually active, or even being physically intimate. For some men (and women), sex is a physical activity that is largely used to fulfill a carnal or physiological need. For those individuals, the person with whom they engage in sexual activities is often negligible, and *never* a chore. For other individuals, sex is the manifestation of feelings and emotions that flow from the brain (often described as our largest sex organ). In the latter group, sex is not enjoyable unless it is with a partner for whom there are genuine feelings, and a partner who demonstrates some reciprocal, genuinely loving feelings for them.

On the far end of the other side of the spectrum, there are individuals who are very uncomfortable with the idea of having sex (perhaps with the exception of the purpose of procreation). For them, sex could be a chore. In between these extremes, there are individuals with a variety of comfort levels with being sexual. Some people do not want to be seen naked (but will have sex). Some people do not generally want to be rubbed, caressed, or snuggled. They do not like having their space invaded, even for the purpose of intercourse. Knowing when and how to have sex with this latter group of individuals would be a challenge. Again, for some of them, if their partner fails the challenge of knowing the optimal time to engage them in sex, sex could be a chore.

Recall the laundry list I provided of reasons why some people get married in the first place. (See essay 2: "The 'Too Picky' Fallacy.") Some of those reasons do not necessarily equate to compatibility (and arguably *true* love). Some examples are getting married because their mate looks good next to them, or their mate has attributes that will serve the union well (e.g., money, power, social status). Often when those attributes are the driving force behind the union, the union itself is actually very shallow, having limited strength on which to build a quality relationship. How then do we think that there would be a quality sex life between two people in such a union when the union itself is so shallow? If both people view sex as strictly filling a carnal need, then the sex might be adequate, or even very good. However, at some point, if one of the spouses finds a true connection outside of the marriage (a very likely scenario), then the sex life inside of the marriage will become less fulfilling for that person, making it even more of a strictly physical act. If that is the case, there would be limited, if any regard, for the feelings and needs of the other spouse. When the spouse being cheated on is summoned to fulfill the now *purely* physical duty, that spouse will likely sense or know that his or her mate would prefer being with someone else. It is then highly possible that the cheated-on spouse would feel that sex is a chore.

Let's say for the sake of argument that we look at individuals who generally like sex, and furthermore, their sexual activity is primarily limited to individuals with whom they feel a genuine connection. When these individuals contemplate sex with their partners, they have euphoric feelings about the act and have no problem engaging in it.

What about when that connection is lost for whatever reason (infidelity, selfishness, narcissism, greed, or stubbornness)? Would someone who is experiencing this negative behavior from his or her partner still remain enthusiastic about having sex? I dare say that unless the negative behavior changed for the better, he or she ultimately would not.

What about couples that are headed toward divorce but still engage in sex? (They abound!) Is it realistic to believe that one of the partners in this type of "arrangement" would not feel that sex has become a chore? After all, some of the negative experiences that lead to divorce—selfishness, neglect, insensitivity—can be the same behaviors that characterize the sex act.

And what of those legions of couples that have troubled relationships but will not "cut bait"? (See essay 40: "Cutting Bait.") Do we really want to delude ourselves into believing that of the two people who are "stuck" in a loveless, unfulfilled marriage or relationship, but who occasionally engage in sex, at least one of the partners feels that sometimes sex is a chore? One of the most liberating feelings in the world as a never-married individual is knowing that sex is not a chore because you are not tethered to someone who does not fulfill your sexual needs.

PART 4

THE HOLIDAYS

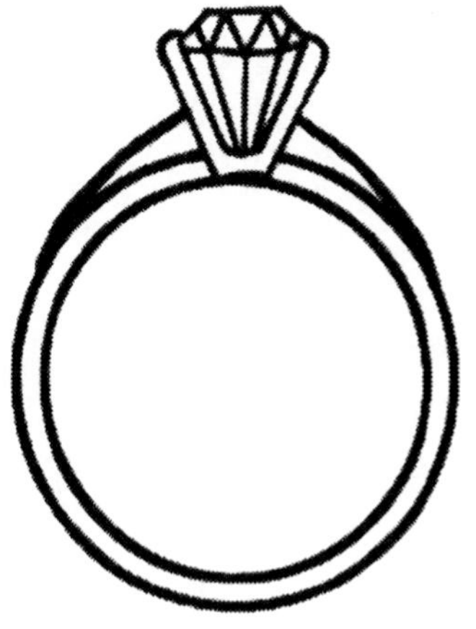

ESSAY 30

HOLIDAY COMPANIONSHIP–A TRUE TEST

One of the hidden *codes* in the world of single individuals is behavior around the holidays. The "holiday" period in this regard spans from late October (pre-Thanksgiving) through Valentine's Day (the middle of February). Single people understand that people's behavior around these holidays can have at least two extremes. On the one hand, there are those who do not want to be perceived as being "committed" to someone during this season and avoid being attached during this time. Even some of the individuals who have already been "involved" will find a reason for breaking off an existing relationship so as not to be attached. In a similar regard, more frugal individuals who are single avoid being hitched during this time because they do not want to be obligated to provide gifts or engage in religious rituals with someone else's family.

On the other hand, there are those individuals who want to have "built-in" companionship for the holidays. These individuals want to have someone to snuggle up to during the cold evenings of Thanksgiving, Christmas, New Year's Eve, and Valentine's Day. What's more, these individuals are paranoid about being viewed as undesirable in front of holiday revelers who have dates. These individuals intensify their search for a partner during this holiday period. The caution with this group is that once the holiday season has passed, or the weather breaks, spring fever sets in and they want their freedom back.

This latter group also contributes to the "sand to the beach" syndrome. It has always been baffling to me that people who say they are looking for love will grab a casual acquaintance or feign interest in someone for the sake of appearances at a social function. The problem there is that the opportunity to meet *new* people is short-circuited.

For those young people becoming increasingly familiar with what being single is like, and to those older individuals just getting back into the dating scene, beware!

ESSAY 31

HOLIDAY LONELINESS

This topic was suggested by Derrick Davis.

How single people (particularly women) feel around the holidays continues to be an ongoing dilemma for some. Holidays can heighten a variety of emotions for a variety of people for a variety of reasons. The feeling of loneliness can certainly be exaggerated during this time.

During the holidays, individuals who desire to be in a relationship but are not in one can be particularly sensitive. At a basic level, the outward appearance of people in relationships is that they are happy and content. Even if these couples are not happy, they are at least assumed to have some level of companionship during the holidays.

In addition, women often experience increased pressure around the holidays from their families. The holidays often mean family gatherings. These fellowships, attended by married family members and their children, often spawn conversations regarding the marital status of the single females in the family. These single female family members can face questions regarding their desire to be married, their ability to attract a man who is interested in them, and their desire to have children.

The potential for feeling lonely around the holidays or facing an inquisition by family members are the undesired characteristics of an impending holiday. I recall that years ago I was anticipating an upcoming Valentine's Day during one of those times when I did not have a significant other. Although my preference would have been to have a date for Cupid's day, I had grown accustomed to surviving the day alone during the periods when I was not involved with someone. This particular year, a group of my girlfriends had the idea that we would get together at one of their homes and cook dinner for ourselves. (This was years before "Galentine's Day" was coined.) I don't mind confessing that this arrangement was not what I had in mind for Valentine's Day, but I thought that the proposed evening's activities was preferred over doing nothing, so I went along with the idea somewhat begrudgingly.

I must say that even to this day, that "girls' night" for Valentine's Day is an occasion that still resonates with me as being one that was quite favorably memorable. I learned a number of lessons that night. First, although having a date was my preference for the evening, being surrounded by good company in general was quite cathartic. Second, being around people who celebrate my strengths and my character is always a good thing, no matter the occasion. Although I would not want to spend every Valentine's Day doing a girls night activity and not having a date, the occasion on which I did just that was a great lesson for me. As we face any impending holiday season, I urge women to take a page from my Galentine's Day experience. First take inventory of the numerous reasons you have to be thankful and the great potential you have for adding value to someone else's life. Then surround yourself with people who celebrate your goodness. If there are any loved ones or true friends in your life, spending time with them will be fulfilling.

It is important to recognize that the so-called happy unions we think we see are not necessarily authentic in their bliss. Some of these unions are contrived just for appearances, especially around special occasions.

ESSAY 32

WHERE WILL WE SPEND THE HOLIDAYS?

It is obvious that one of the benefits of having a spouse is that there is built-in companionship. Hence there should be no question regarding that companionship during the holiday season. The irony is that the issue of how and where holidays will be spent can become one of the most highly contentious aspects of a marriage or committed relationship.

I once had a colleague who declared that irrespective of his marital status, his holidays would *always* be spent with *his* mother. His declaration became another one of those moments that would forever shape my perception of what constitutes a happy marriage. When he made that pronouncement, I instantly asked myself, what if his spouse felt the same way about her mother? What if their mothers lived in separate cities that were far apart, making it logistically impossible to share the same holiday with both mothers? What if he and his wife had children? Would there ever be Christmas celebrations at *their home* with their children in any given year?

As one who is extremely family oriented, spending holidays with my family has always been a highlight of my year. However, I have always been mindful that when I have a significant other, I negotiate on "where" I spend my holidays. (The "one" for me wants to share the holidays with me. Therefore, where "we" spend the holidays will always require careful consideration.) I was fully prepared to sacrifice some holidays with my family in some years in order to be with my significant other at *his* family's house, which might not have been in close proximity to my family. Ironically, I have seen more couples locked in a stalemate over where holidays will be spent. To me this rigidity speaks to something that goes far beyond the issue of the holidays.

PART 5

CHILDREN AND RELATIONSHIPS

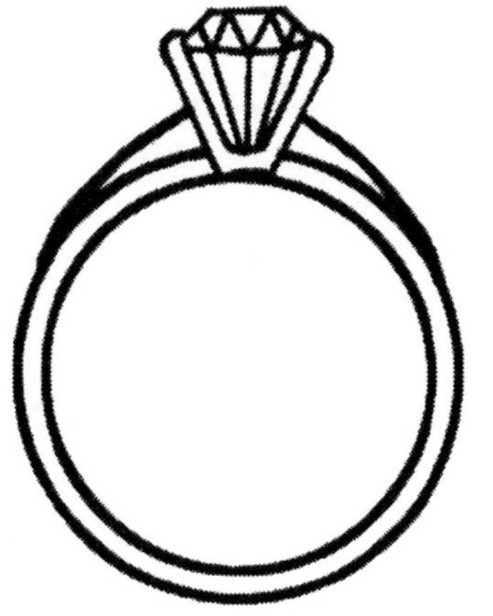

ESSAY 33

CHILDREN ARE A BLESSING, PERIOD!

As I contemplated this book in general and this essay in particular, I found it excruciatingly important that I explicitly state my belief that a child is always, always a blessing, period!

That said, the fact is that one of the top reasons for the failure of second marriages is the dynamic of incorporating children.[1] This fact is reflected in the observation that special care must be taken when incorporating children from a previous union into a subsequent relationship heading toward marriage. Again, let me be clear that *children are a blessing*! Their parents' navigation in a postseparation relationship is not the children's problem, fault, or responsibility.

People who are dating often want their love interests to adjust their lives to the established relationship, routines, patterns, and characteristics of an existing or preexisting family structure. When it comes to children (and the dating dynamic), some people want their love interests to retrofit themselves into an existing pattern of living. In that regard, it appears that instead of moving forward and creating something new, some individuals want to preserve an existence that has been irreparably dismantled by divorce, separation, or a nonexistent union in the first place. (Please note that I do not advocate that a man or woman should make major adjustments in their lives, especially with respect to their children, during a time when they are just getting to know a love interest

1 Jill Brooke, "Marry Again? Nine Reasons Divorced Women Choose Not To," More.Com, December 16, 2009, https://www.firstwivesworld.com/index.php/resources-articles/item/5076-marry-again-nine-reasons-divorced-women-choose-not-to.

or during a courtship. I speak of adjustments that should be made when a marriage is imminent.)

Many single parents often endeavor to create a seamless environment for their child with respect to the transformation from a predivorce to a postdivorce lifestyle. This is perhaps possible when neither parent has remarried. However, in the case whereby a parent is remarrying, how can pure seamlessness exist? In this regard, on a spiritual level, there is no footnote regarding any other influences that negate the notion of "two people becoming one" in marriage, even when children from a previous union are part of the scenario. I understand that for most responsible parents, their children are their lives, and their children come first. I am simply stating that if one wants to tout the tenets of many religions and subsequently claim to make a covenant before God to "cleave unto their partner," one cannot have it both ways.

This is not to say that children should not be of *paramount* importance in all considerations in a relationship. However, children have often moved beyond importance to superiority, or worst case, the singular factor in all decisions. It is important for individuals to be honest with themselves with respect to whether having a new spouse is practical for them given their individual philosophy about how they want to raise their children.

Following are observations on the subject:

- A parent's relationship with his or her child and the child's opinion virtually always trump the relationship with a new spouse.
- Disciplinary issues with the child are off limits to the new spouse.
- The children's needs (often "wants") *always* come first, no matter what.
- Opinions regarding physical maintenance of the child are off limits to the new spouse (e.g., standards for hairstyles, clothing styles, homework habits).

- The child is as much a *surrogate mate* as he or she is offspring (this is not suggesting any type of incestuous relationship).

Conversely, it is only fair to acknowledge that some individuals enter into a marriage whereby their new spouse has children from a previous union, but they are not honest about where their heart is with respect to taking on the responsibilities of parenting someone else's children. This lack of honesty and sincerity, in my opinion, is particularly egregious. If one is not willing to love and take responsibility for the "total family package," then one should not marry someone who has children.

Children did not ask to be born into this world. Children are not pawns to be shuffled around at the whim of individuals who do not take the responsibility of having children as seriously as they should. When we contemplate life-altering decisions (e.g., getting married, having children, getting divorced), we need to be ever mindful of the effect those decisions have on everyone involved. That effect has numerous tentacles, and it lasts a lifetime.

ESSAY 34

BOYS AND BOOKS

WHEN I WAS an adolescent, I remember one of my mother's mantras, "Boys and books don't mix." There were two main messages in this admonition. The first message was that "books" (a euphemism for getting an education) needed to be a key focus of my formative years. Getting a good education was a core standard in our household. The minimum standard became getting a college degree. (Neither of my parents had been formally educated beyond high school.)

My mother also understood that an essential aspect of being prepared to pursue a college degree was having a sound K–12 education foundation. Getting that grounding meant being focused on "the books." Boys could distract me from that focus. The thought was that if I became overenamored with boys without being grounded in education fundamentals, it would not bode well for me and my future successes.

There are volumes of literature on the interactions between boys and girls (more specifically sexual encounters) that can set a trajectory for both that is arguably contradictory to setting those boys and girls on an optimal path to a productive and fulfilling life. At a basic level, it is fair to say that adolescents are in no position to take care of themselves, let alone a spouse, child, or overall family unit. Hence it is reasonable that adolescents be advised to have as their primary focus the advancement of their education as opposed to "mating" with another individual.

The "boys and books" concept, when thought of as strictly pertaining to the interaction between boys and girls (absent any physical sexual interaction), has much to consider. The notion is that the energy of the infatuation between the two becomes a force unto itself that can dominate both individuals' thoughts and trump their having focus on anything else (e.g., education). Inherent in this mental and emotional attention to one another also is that under the best of circumstances, the emotional investment can quickly turn into a major problem if things do not go well. Certainly if the relationship were to go horribly wrong (e.g., cheating, abuse), the "boys and books" admonition takes even more of a precipitous negative effect on the girl (or boy).

When the "boys and books" scenario transforms into the ultimate complication (the conception of a child), both the boy and girl are irrevocably changed (irrespective of whether the pregnancy is carried to term).

ESSAY 35

BABIES AND BOOKS

(Please first read essay 33: "Children Are a Blessing, Period!" and essay 34: "Boys and Books.")

If "Boys and Books" are a challenging combination, "babies and books" are even more of a complication. When a baby has entered into the lives of young people at a point when, by most standards, the boy and girl are not equipped mentally, emotionally, and financially to handle it, the trajectory for their lives moves in a direction that can create a set of circumstances that hinders other areas of their lives. (Note: Fortunately, in many circumstances family and extended family step in to mitigate adverse effects.)

Now the conventional progression through various stages of life is altered. Neither party is a "free agent" any longer. Every life decision the boy and girl make moving forward in their lives is forever tied to their new child and the child's other parent. (Read essay 39: "Grown Children: An Oxymoron.") These newly minted parents must (or should) incorporate their child into every aspect of their lives. This is not to say that they cannot have lives with great trajectories. However, they will have to make concessions that otherwise do not characterize a young person's life.

Many never-married, childless individuals have a keen understanding of the potential tribulations of marrying wrong, having a baby with the wrong lifetime partner (spouse), or worse, having a baby with a temporary partner (or spouse). We have intuited that if it is very challenging to find an optimal mate, having a baby with a suboptimal mate makes life that much more complicated. Furthermore, doing so during a time when one's own life is in the midst of dependency on a parent or guardian, is worse. And again, irrespective of whether the two individuals marry, they are irrevocably tied to each other because of the child.

Certainly having a baby as a teen has obvious shortcomings, given that in most cases the teen is still considered a minor, or at the very least is not in the best position to take care of herself in basic ways. Having a baby for which you must be the prime provider and caretaker when you have not accomplished your education objectives (or established an alternative for economic viability) is even more exacerbating.

Babies do not honor your need to be in class (or handle the wide variety of assignments and tasks that need to be accomplished outside of class). Babies do not honor your need to finance the tools of your education (e.g., books, computer). Babies do not honor your need to participate in or attend the kinds of functions or activities that lead to gainful employment (e.g., employer receptions, job fairs, interviews). "Babies and books" do not mix!

In today's environment, where a college education is becoming the basic standard for having a fighting chance for being able to take care of oneself, attending college is obviously essential. In our current environment, the cost of higher education is steadily escalating, assistance for financing that education is constantly ebbing and flowing if not downright declining, and educational quality in too many arenas is declining. The convergence of these facts makes attaining a college degree more difficult than ever. Adding a baby to that mix, on a foundation that is unsteady, is not good.

I often point out to students that if purchasing books for their classes is a challenge, how can they afford a baby?

ESSAY 36

MY CHILDREN WOULD HAVE HATED ME, SAID OPRAH WINFREY

Approaching her sixtieth birthday, Oprah Winfrey said that had she had children, they would most likely have hated her. She made this statement based on the fact that she has led a professional life that has been *exceptionally* dynamic and demanding. She believes that the focus and attention that has been required for her to achieve the type of success she has achieved has meant that some things have had to suffer. With respect to her thoughts on having children, she stated, "They would have ended up on the equivalent of the *Oprah* show talking about me because something [in my life] would have had to suffer, and it would've probably been them."[1] (Note: I draw a distinction between living the kind of life Oprah has had versus having a professional life that has a fraction of the demands that are on Oprah's life.)

Oprah's sentiment spurred thoughts I have had over the years regarding having children. Like the desire I have always had to be married, I have always had the desire to have children. The ways in which I have contemplated having children have followed a similar pattern of critical thinking that I have applied to the idea of getting married.

Years ago, a professional working *married* female made a comment that would become a lightning rod for my thoughts on the subject of having children. This female had two minor children (a girl and a boy)

---

1 Michael Rothman, "Oprah Winfrey Reveals Why She Never Had Children," ABC News Blogs, December 12, 2013, http://abcnews.go.com/blogs/entertainment/2013/12/oprah-winfrey-reveals-why-she-never-had-children/.

at the time. The two children were contemplating their extracurricular activities (outside of school). Her directive to them was that they had to choose one activity that they could both share. This was a requirement based arguably on the fact that she did not have time to chauffer them to two different activities. (Note: She was in a middle-class family. This was not a case of two parents working two jobs to make ends meet.)

My immediate thought at the time was that the requirement she levied on her two children to "share" an activity was woefully inequitable to her children. I think of the countless individuals who have risen to extraordinary heights with their skills based on the development of those skills in their youth (e.g., Michael Jordan, Beyoncé, Michael Phelps, Dakota Fanning, Ron Howard). Furthermore, given that the woman had a boy and a girl, I thought that her requirement that they had to "share an activity" was particularly unfair to them. What if each child liked activities that were stereotypically gender based (e.g., football versus ballet)? Honestly, my thought was, if she did not have the time to support her children in this basic way (shuttling the children to one extracurricular activity apiece), was having more than one child a wise choice?

These sentiments also raise for me the ongoing issue of the degree to which, all too often, the person largely responsible for the welfare of the children in an "intact" marriage is the wife. The woman in my example was married and still with her husband. It seems to be the case that irrespective of how intense a woman's professional life is, she is assigned the lion's share of responsibility for the children. All too often, whether a woman is a stay-at-home mom or the CFO of a major company, she has chief responsibility for the "second shift" (postwork, domestic, and child-care duties). It still seems apparent that there is a preponderance of husbands who need to step it up. I salute those working moms who work tirelessly to make life *reasonable* for all their loved ones (and hopefully themselves as well).

ESSAY 37

ELF ON A SHELF: AN ODE TO MEN

TODAY'S MATRIMONIAL UNIONS will likely involve "blended" families. That is, a man and woman are likely to bring children from previous relationships into the newly formed family. These unions face a set of challenges that are uniquely characteristic of blended families. Men and women alike often have moments of mentally reverting to a time and space that is reflective of the way life used to be, before divorce became the "new normal." In that regard, the children who are a part of the new configuration are sometimes afforded a status that is atypical of that of children's roles in conventional family units.

A case in point is that the male children of some women get elevated to a form of manhood prematurely, because postdivorce, postseparation, or simply the absence of a "man" in the family structure has often made male children become the men in the household. When the mothers of these male children subsequently connect with an authentic adult man, this can pose a challenge to the relationship between women and their adult suitors.

There are myriad combinations of the dynamics among a woman, her male child, and her new love interest. In a conventional family, a male child is subject to the directives of his mother and father. When a man joins a woman and her son (in this example, for the purpose of marriage), convention is not always the order of the day. Often the woman expects her betrothed to "get in where he can fit in" with respect to the established routine of her and her son. On occasion, this can also translate into the new husband or stepfather having a limited voice (if any) or control over the actions of the male child. Many women form a bit of a partition between the relationships they have with their sons and the relationship they have with their companions. (This dynamic can also hold true for a man with a new wife, and the dynamics that can exist for a child of any gender.)

What becomes a bit inequitable is when the woman seeks and enjoys her new husband's financial "sponsorship" of the entire family unit (including the male child from a previous union), but wants to limit the new husband's voice. Men are not elves to be used at will and then placed back on a shelf. When women seek a matrimonial union with a new man, they should be honest about their feelings regarding the holistic aspects of the union, vis-à-vis the children they bring into the union.

ESSAY 38

LOVING YOUR CHILD, DISRESPECTING ME

WITHIN THE MOST optimal relationships between a man and a woman, bringing a child into the unit tends to alter the dynamics. That is, the child often becomes the focal point of the relationship. In many scenarios, the relationship between the child and either parent is stronger than the relationship between the parents. Imagine what happens between a parent and child whose relationship is stronger than the one between the two parents when the parents break up. In other words, the parent-child relationship often trumps any other relationship that comes into existence. Add to that fact the introduction of a new mate (other than the biological parent) to one of the parents. Often that new mate stands no chance of building an impenetrable bond with his or her love interest. Reportedly, "...the biggest reason for second marriage breakups, according to the Stepfamily Foundation, is because of [a] kid not getting along with their parent's new love interest and their children."[1]

This is often the scenario that an individual gets introduced to when entering a relationship with a divorced person. If the new couple marries, the stepparent often is not afforded the rights and privileges to "parent" the child, as is comparable to that of a biological parent. This spells trouble on a number of levels.

It is not practical to think that a mature parental figure is not afforded jurisdiction over the parenting of a minor child who resides under his or her roof. In the case of a stepfather, a woman often wants

1 Jill Brooke, "Marry Again? Nine Reasons Divorced Women Choose Not To," More.Com, December 16, 2009, https://www.firstwivesworld.com/index.php/resources-articles/item/5076-marry-again-nine-reasons-divorced-women-choose-not-to.

an adult male figure in her life, and she wants that male figure to love unconditionally, provide and protect, yet she does not want that same adult male figure to weigh in on issues related to her biological son from a previous union.

When men and women split up and a child is involved, the child often becomes the surrogate mate. Hence the child gets elevated to a status higher than that of "child." Subsequently, when an adult partner (a rival) gets introduced to the parent-child dynamic, a problem potentially arises in that the "rival" adult is not subsequently afforded the status of having stewardship over the minor child.

ESSAY 39

GROWN CHILDREN: AN OXYMORON

OFTEN, WHEN PEOPLE are becoming acquainted with a would-be romantic interest, they qualify that they have children with the statement, "My children are grown." This is intended to signal that if a romantic relationship developed, the love interest need not be concerned about considering the responsibility of "minor" children.

Anyone who truly understands what "family" exemplifies, understands that *children do not come with expiration dates.* I am reminded of someone with whom I was getting to know, who at first told me that he did not have children at all, only to reference a grandson in a conversation days later. (Needless to say, science has yet to create grandchildren who were not the offspring of one's children.) It turned out that my acquaintance obviously had kids (hence the grandson). In fact, at one point, the grandson had been sent to live with him during some weeks over a particular summer because the child needed some discipline and stability at the time.

My acquaintance justified the fraudulent nature of his earlier declaration regarding not having kids by saying that he had essentially been estranged from his children. The reality of misrepresenting the facts about having kids was unsettling to me to say the least, since my question to him regarding having children was not, "Do you have children, and furthermore, do you have healthy relationships with them?" The question had simply been, "Do you have children?"

The subsequent "reference" to a grandson who had lived with him for a summer proved one of the many sentiments I have regarding the "plain and simple fact" of someone having kids. In his particular case, although my acquaintance had been estranged from his children, his grandson at one point needed the stability and financial and emotional support of a responsible adult. The person who fulfilled that role was his grandfather. This scenario exemplified that it is highly possible (more likely probable), across the lives of children and grandchildren, that they will need some substantive support from their parent or grandparent when they are well into adulthood. That support might be financial, emotional, or caretaking.

Unlike some people who have children who once grown become shifted to a category of "children but not really," many of us unmarried (no kids) types understand better than most that children do not have expiration dates. Sure, the natural order of things suggests that when children reach an age of majority (likely 21), they should be well involved in a lifestyle that is liberated from the supervision, caretaking, and otherwise responsibility of their parents. Hence, if their parents become romantically involved with someone other than the child's other biological parent, that someone should not fear that they might need to consider taking on the types of responsibilities that go along with rearing a minor child.

An earlier essay (essay 12: "The 'Footnote' Wife") intimated, in part, that many individuals become separated, divorced, or widowed and approach subsequent romantic relationships as mere amendments to a life that largely has already been lived. They believe, and often function, as if the two lives can largely remain separate, with limited integration. That new life with a new love often operates in an existence predicated on the new love being an appendage to a previous life, not a new life that is integrated into the past. Hence the "grown children" concept suggests that the "children" are part of a past that does not have to factor into a subsequent romantic relationship.

I find it troublesome for both the children of a preexisting union and the romantic interest of a subsequent union to be thought of à la carte. A family is a family is a family. It might not be bonded by blood, but there should be a desire for seeking unity, harmony, and togetherness in a way that works as optimally as possible.

Grandchildren become the sobering influence that should have people realizing that children do not become historical figures. Likewise, untimely health and financial challenges present that same sobering reality. If someone's adult child were to become stricken with a debilitating illness or befall some financial hardship, I would hope that his or her parents would be first in line to lend assistance to the best degree possible. If the parent has a new love (and I dare say more than just a love, a new spouse), that new love is undeniably affected and often involved, whether anyone wants to acquiesce to that fact or not.

Unless one has completely and permanently severed himself from his children, there will be countless potential conditions and occasions where the new love will cross paths with those children. (Note: A parent separating himself from his child does not mean the child will not one day seek out that parent.) At the very least, basic activities such as family and holiday gatherings or graduations and weddings will bring this about. In addition, as previously stated, more substantive interactions based on life hardships will most certainly force crossed paths and involvement, or at least sacrifice, from the new love. Therefore, "the children being grown" is simply a chronological age description, because they are still "the children."

PART 6

BREAKUPS

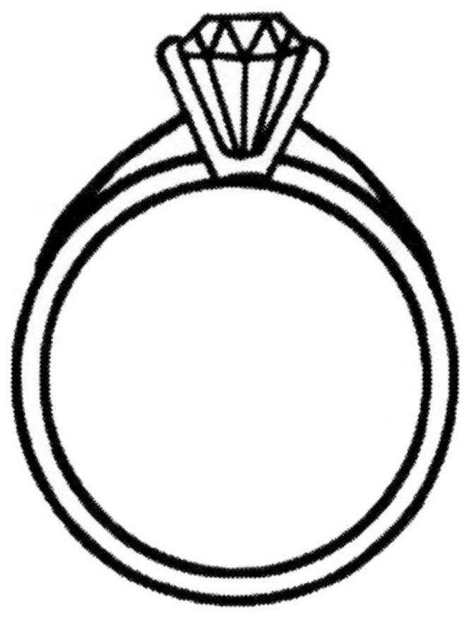

ESSAY 40

CUTTING BAIT

When we ring in a new year, that year brings with it the promise of a life ahead that perhaps eclipses the year or years behind us. We are often beaming with the possibilities of the ways in which life might be just a little kinder to us in the year ahead, and that some of the discontent of the past can be washed away in that new year. Romance often tops the wish list for what we want in the brand new year. Contrarily, we often want the benefit of the new possibilities while holding on to the ways (and people) of the past that have not served us well. This fact reminds me of one of my fishing trips.

I have been fishing a couple of times in my life, and ironically, both times have been deep sea fishing. I recall that this type of fishing required me to be anchored to a seat in the back of a boat by way of a special jacket, with the fishing rod holstered into the seat. I remember that on one of the fishing trips, I had caught a strong fish that was "running." (Running is when a fish has bitten the line and swims at breakneck speed away from the boat.) I, with the help of crew members on the boat, struggled to catch that fish for a solid twenty minutes or more, trying to reel the fish into the boat. I am happy to report that we ultimately won, and finally reeled the fish to the side of the boat. (Had we needed to fight much longer, we would have cut the bait or line.) Once reeled to the side, the fish continued to battle for its life, still resisting being caught. One of the crew members had to club the fish over the head a couple of times before it could be hauled into the boat. Many men and women are "struggling" with mates who are functioning just like my fish, running away from the boat while taking the bait and fishing line with them. The fish was justified in trying to get as far away from the boat as it could because for it, the alternative was not in its best interests. Unfortunately, individuals in some relationships exhibit behavior that is similar to that running fish. Often an individual can manage to wrangle a mate to the boat (relationship), but then the person who was wrangled has to be "clubbed" (psychologically) to cooperate in the relationship. (Note: I am not speaking of scenarios of domestic violence. I speak of situations whereby individuals do everything they can to coerce someone into staying in relationships that his or her partner has determined [for whatever reason] are not in his or her best interest.)

When we "hang around" in relationships with people about whom we are constantly finding reasons to complain and with whom we are consistently unhappy, and they are "running away from the boat," it is time to make a real break. It is time to cut bait. (The exception would be when counseling helps.) If you are spending weeks, months, and sometimes years complaining about the same person regarding the same behavior you despise (wrangling), you are cosigning your own misery. Conversely, if you are constantly allowing yourself to be the object of wrangling, you are a coconspirator.

Some men believe that moaning and groaning are simply a part of a woman's DNA. Hence, if she is constantly griping, over time, what he hears is very much akin to the adult dialogue in Charlie Brown episodes (i.e., wah, wah…). And truthfully, if a person is complaining about the same thing over and over and not ending the relationship, his or her mate has no motivation to actually process the complaint and negotiate a solution. People must learn to make a clean break from a relationship that is not working well for them, hence moving on with their lives. Staying in a bad relationship can signal that the relationship is not as bad as the complaining person makes it out to be. Sometimes the party "at fault" does not "get it" until the relationship is terminated. I have learned that sometimes the only thing people hear are feet (walking out of a relationship).

ESSAY 41

CUTTING BAIT TWO-LESSONS LEARNED FROM MOVING ON

I RECALL VERY vividly the euphoria I felt in a relationship I had in my early adult life with someone with whom I felt I was truly in love. I felt my search was over and that I need not look any more for the man with whom I would spend the rest of my life.

Breaking off that relationship was a painful experience. I thought it impossible to ever replace the chemistry I had with him. The fact was, replacing that chemistry was indeed not going to happen. However, the revelation in that was that I needed to learn what was meant by building new chemistry.

For months after the dissolution of our relationship, I was looking for someone to insert in his place. I was looking for the carbon copy of that relationship. I had to make myself realize that there were reasons that we were no longer together; therefore, I did not need, nor should I have been seeking, a carbon copy.

As I have grown older and have had a few relationships since that time, I have come to realize the beauty in identifying how the chemistry of a new love mixes with mine. You cannot go back, nor should you want to. As a case in point, the coach of the US Women's Olympic basketball team spoke of the fact that although the United States has won gold medals in six straight Olympics, every team has been different. Each team had to explore its unique characteristics, talents, and weaknesses that could be leveraged as a unit for the goal of achieving gold.

New opportunities for relationships come into our lives for a reason. We are unable to have the beauty in those new opportunities manifest if we are holding on to the past. Besides, isn't that "past" the past for a reason? In many cases, didn't we recognize that there were reasons for why we needed to move on? Those lessons provide the backdrop for why we truly need not go through life constantly peering into our rearview mirrors.

I have come to appreciate the ways in which the chemistry of my relationship with one person is different from my chemistry with someone else. This discovery has served me well during those times when I realize that it is time to simply move on, or cut bait.

ESSAY 42

THE UNENGAGED: A SECRET SOCIETY

I RECALL THAT about twenty-five years ago, I received a very neatly, professionally printed postcard in the mail that simply read, "The marriage between *x* and *y* will not take place." At first I was baffled because the card was so elegantly done, so the somewhat disappointing news it bore was a bit of a contradiction. My confusion quickly turned to gratitude for the tasteful (and timely) way in which this not-so-pleasant news was communicated. Little did I know that, within a few years, I would be living the unengaged experience.

More than twenty years ago, I was engaged to be married. My fiancé was my absolute best friend in the world, and I was thrilled about the infinite ways in which living out the rest of my life with him would be fulfilling. Like other blissfully happy, engaged women, I had set plans in motion for the big day of our nuptials. My wedding party participants were established, the venues for the ceremony and the reception were secure, and many of the vendors had been contracted. Planning for the upcoming wedding had taken on a life of its own, and it seemed everything in the universe was pointed toward that day. Unfortunately, "irreconcilable differences" between my fiancé and me forced the termination of the engagement.

Needless to say, the broken engagement phase was not a happy time for me. However, this was a time with at least one tremendous revelation. The revelation was that there is an entire society of unengaged individuals who are in our midst but of whom we are unaware. These souls are *not* going out of their way to hide their pasts. The fact is simply that discussions regarding past wedding engagements are not frequently had. The subject is also not top of mind for those of us who have experienced broken engagements. (Perhaps this is a testimony to the peace that settles in regarding the decision once the disappointment and heartache have dissipated.) This also underscores that moving past a broken engagement is far easier than negotiating one's way out of a failed marriage.

That this unengaged group is not readily identifiable creates a misconception about the frequency with which the decision to not go through with a wedding is made. There are countless women and men who have been brides and grooms "to be" who, for a variety of reasons, opted to abort wedding plans. I truly believe that if more people were aware that calling off a wedding is not a completely alien concept, more men and women would feel empowered to make that decision when appropriate to do so.

Many failed marriages could have been averted if there simply had been the courage to call off weddings that were already destined to be troubled marriages. There is life after a broken engagement. Family and friends do get over the termination of wedding plans. And if those loved ones are slow to get over the change, in time they have no choice. More importantly, going through with a wedding (and therefore a marriage) that should not have taken place in the first place has far more long-term pain associated with it than the short-term "inconvenience" of calling off a wedding or the short-term discomfort of someone who is not the one getting married. A wedding is for a day (perhaps longer depending on culture). A marriage is intended to be for a lifetime. Moving forward with plans for a day's activities is downright foolhardy if the lifetime that follows is destined for heartache.

ESSAY 43

"YOU'RE STILL YOU"-SURVIVING THE PAIN OF A BREAKUP

"YOU'RE STILL YOU," were the words Dana Reeve spoke to her husband, Christopher Reeve (a.k.a. Superman) days after he was thrown from a horse, causing his spinal cord injury and subsequent paralysis.[1] He had lost a great deal of self-confidence and felt that since his physical condition was severely altered, he was not as valuable to her anymore.

How does this relate to being "happily never married"? The way Dana Reeve reassured her husband that he was still the man he was when she married him is similar to the way a person who has suffered a breakup needs to reassure himself or herself that the breakup is a circumstance in life, not an alteration of character. Unfortunately, many people tend to internalize breakups. Women in particular are sometimes inclined to assign negative attributes to their self-worth as a result of a breakup.

It is helpful for people to realize that a breakup is not to be identified as losing those favorable characteristics about you that make you desirable. Instead, remind yourself that all the goodness and positive factors about you that were present when you entered the relationship are still there when the relationship has ended. We also need to understand that breakups happen to almost everyone at some point. Those who have learned to navigate beyond breakups understand that although there will always be other people who are prettier or more handsome, smarter,

1 Kim Bates, "You're Still You—Christopher Reeve," Chicken Soup Stories, April 9, 2012, www.chicken-soup-stories.blogspot.in/2012/04/youre-still-you-christopher-reeve.html.

better educated, wealthier, healthier, and so on; they too experience breakups. Most of us are not immune.

The only thing that has changed when we experience a breakup is that the *relationship* has ended. That is it. That is all! Make no mistake, we are not "less than" because we are no longer in the relationship. To put this in perspective, think of your favorite musical group. There might be times when that group is momentarily out of the public eye. That does not mean that you no longer value and thoroughly enjoy the music they have already made. As a matter of fact, their absence from the mainstream perhaps intensifies your love for their talent. They are still your favorite. The degree of *public* attention on that musical group at any moment does not alter your affinity for them.

Unfortunately, particularly in the case of women, there are some instances when they experience breakups and their former mates subsequently belittle them or make them feel they are nothing without them. Women need to understand that they are still themselves postbreakup ("you're still you"). What one particular man did not recognize and appreciate in a woman, *another man will* in due time. The key is that women need to gather the strength within and garner support from friends and family to get past the pain. Most importantly, if a woman is being belittled by an ex, that ex is demonstrating why he should be an ex. Mean-spirited character assassination is a form of bullying, irrespective of whether it is born out of hurt from a breakup.

What is important is that men and women do not allow an erosion of their self-esteem or self-worth. An unpleasant part of the cycle of life is the disappointment caused by breakups. To paraphrase a cliché, the rain in our lives helps us better appreciate the sunshine. When the person who is truly *worthy* of you comes along, you will be in an even better position to appreciate them after surviving the heartache of a breakup.

ESSAY 44

WHY LIVE THE SECOND HALF OF LIFE IN MISERY?

IT IS NOT uncommon to run across couples that have been married for twenty years or more who seemingly are "suddenly" getting a divorce. The first time I witnessed this I was in my twenties. From my perspective at the time, the couple may as well have been married for a lifetime. Of course the truth for me was that they had been married nearly *my* entire lifetime. Realizing that this couple was getting divorced after so many years of being committed to a marriage seemed unconscionable to me.

Throughout my lifetime since that point, I have continued to witness people who have been married in excess of twenty years get divorced. As I have grown older, that two-decade cessation remains disheartening to me, but I have gained greater insight into what can happen within a twenty-year time frame. This insight is heightened by repeatedly witnessing the phenomenon.

No one will ever know the nuances that are being experienced in any couple's marriage. However, there are some realizations that can be observed from the outside looking in. Twenty years in the overall scheme of a life span (now pegged to be about seventy-six years) is not an exceptionally long time. It is approximately a fourth of the average lifetime, if one has gotten married in his or her twenties and has been married twenty years, and has nearly half a lifetime or more to live. (Truthfully, once the stress of a bad marriage is well in the rearview mirror, one's life span is probably extended!) I imagine that when the decision is made to cut ties after having put twenty years into a marriage, one of the realizations is that if the marriage has not gained the traction it needs, there is a yearning to live the second half of one's life in a spirit of more harmony.

I think the twenty-first century will continue to witness more of this phenomenon. This will be in part based on the already atrocious divorce rate, as well as the overall ability to connect with a broader world that the proliferation of social media has created. No matter how long we live, it is generally never long enough. Therefore, whatever we can do to maximize happiness in that life span, we should do it, even if that means severing a twenty-plus-year marriage.

PART 7

EPILOGUE

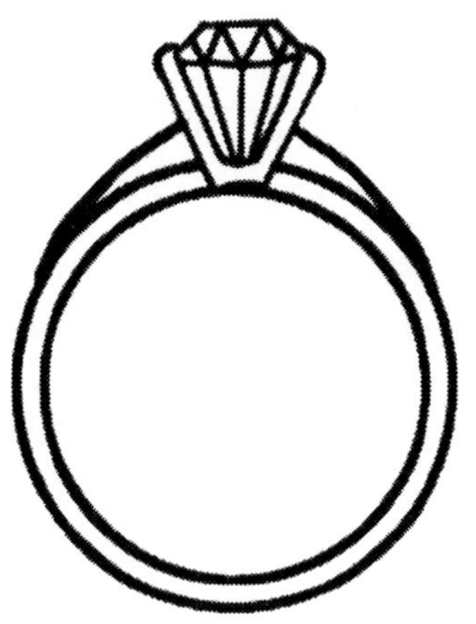

ESSAY 45

SHE BETTER BE ABLE TO COOK!

THIS BOOK STARTED out with an introduction that provided the sobering statistics on divorce and told of the growing rate of single individuals in this country (now more than 50 percent of the adult population). The essays herein describe discrete experiences and observations that have affected my decisions regarding whether I should "take the plunge" into marriage. Essentially, the narrative is that the institution of marriage works well for some but is an abysmal failure (sometimes numerous times) for others. The reasons for some of those failures often start well before the "I dos." Some of the reasons overall for marriage or relationship failure include marrying someone else's choice for you in a mate, marrying to gain financial support for you and your children, the lack of *authentic* companionship, the inability to end relationships that were based on impractical conditions, marrying because of the optics (wanting the "appearance" of being desirable), and marrying to "cure" loneliness.

In spite of the fact that divorce rates generally have worsened over the past fifty years, many people continue to pursue marriage with a sense of it being the gold standard of living. Although I too continue to desire the married lifestyle, I have not allowed others' perceptions that marriage provides a euphoric life existence to cloud my practical judgment on the nature of being married. Instead, I have taken my experiences with courtship and dating at face value, not projecting a reality that I fabricated in my head. All the while, I have not allowed my "single" status to prevent me from continuously enjoying my life.

This last vignette provides a slice-of-life example of why I am still single. It exemplifies that although meeting people is an essential part of ultimately getting married, everyone you meet is not meant for you and should not be transitioned into "marriage" material. Furthermore, the example also illustrates that we have to be particularly vigilant in evaluating who we marry. Although many individuals are quick to label never-married people as "picky," the realities of joining two lives have time and time again proved that marriage evaluation cannot be taken lightly.

Years ago one of my cousins introduced me to one of her bachelor church members. When she introduced me to him, he could barely extend a friendly greeting to me before he belted out, "She better be able to cook!" I was standing right in front of him. Aside from the disrespect of referring to me in the third person while I was in his presence, I thought it was particularly egregious that he thought that bellowing out *his* "requirement" in a mate on first meeting was socially acceptable behavior. Some may say that perhaps I was being hypersensitive over a playful quip. My retort is, given that he repeated himself a few times within a few seconds and still barely addressed me directly. I dare say he was signposting for what would come if I were to entertain getting to know him. (He could have also been exemplifying immediate disinterest in me, for which the end result is still the same. See essay 40 "Cutting Bait", essay 41 "Cutting Bait Two", and essay 43 "You're Still You".)

For the record, I actually can cook well, and at times do so often. Furthermore, I actually prefer cooking when I have someone with whom I can share my culinary skills. As a matter of fact, many of my love interests have themselves been skilled in the kitchen, so I know firsthand how much affinity can be built by having someone cook for you. Although over the years I have developed an increased appreciation for the value that having someone who can cook can bring to a relationship, what I do not appreciate is being "commanded" to cook (or being "commanded" to do *anything* for that matter). This scenario is symbolic of why many women like me have often been "driven to" the never-married status.

The problem I had with the previously mentioned gentleman is that he appeared to have a one-dimensional requirement for simply getting to know someone, let alone getting married. Furthermore, he was downright crude in his communication of that dimension. He was signaling to me that his desires were paramount in his world, and anyone else's needs (which would include a wife one day) were negligible. Although I would prefer that if someone is so staunchly entrenched in his desires that he be honest about it, he clearly had a preference that appeared to be nonnegotiable. Being married to someone who is that dogmatic and rude, for me, would be the very essence of emptiness. I would be lonely in a relationship with him.

Some might suggest that the guy was just having a "moment," in which case I would acquiesce that we were both guilty of being one-dimensional. My experiences and observations, however, have largely proven to me the reality of the Maya Angelou adage, "When someone shows you who they are, believe them." I would add to that, at the very least, keep an eye (and ear) on them. Too often, people turn a blind eye to undesirable behavior and instead search for euphoric benefits they can gain from a relationship. Although this search *can* be fruitful, often it leads right back to where one started. (Note: Over the past thirty years, I can count about only three instances out of the *hundreds* of conversations I have had with individuals headed toward or experiencing divorce in which a contentious issue that led to divorce was not an issue that was *always* a factor in the relationship, present from day one.)

People generally are who they are.* Their persona either works for you or it does not. That the gentleman in my scenario could not pause to have a dialogue with me regarding what I could, or could not, do was troublesome. Furthermore, his seeming lack of interest in my desires

* Although many people tend to be entrenched in who they are, there are some people who are capable of changing and evolving. Often, simply maturing brings about a change in a person. Others change because they gain insights through relationship counseling. Unfortunately, many people often do not change while they are in the relationship with people their adverse behavior affects. The growth (change) occurs once they have moved (or been forced to move) past the relationship, and they have a chance to reflect back and see what they have lost.

(vis-à-vis his nonnegotiable cooking requirement) was also telling. (Guys beware: You can find yourself a good cook. When she tires of your disrespect, she can use her cooking skills to *communicate* her discontent to your stomach.)

I would like to think that I am a kaleidoscope of talent and character waiting to be shared with someone who at the very least will demonstrate the willingness to get to know me. As such, if I were to be with someone who could not see that a relationship is far more than a woman's ability to cook, that would result in an unfulfilling union for me. The *basics* of any relationship include mutual respect, communication, and selflessness. *True* love is hard to grow when it is stifled by the lack of those ingredients. Countless women spend their energies on chasing down men, or being married to men, who have demonstrated limited promise for providing holistic appreciation for who they are and what they bring to a relationship.

ABOUT THE AUTHOR

Dr. Kendra L. Harris is a marketing professor. Prior to her career in higher education, she worked in the area of sales and marketing for the Lincoln Mercury Division of Ford Motor Company. Born and raised in Washington, DC she is the youngest of five siblings and is the only girl. Her parents were married for 68 years and all of her brothers have been married. She has been "officially" engaged, once.

Dr. Harris has taught at the collegiate level for nearly thirty years. She is currently an associate professor of marketing in the College of Business and Public Affairs at Alabama A&M University in Huntsville, AL, teaching both undergraduate and graduate courses. Prior to joining the faculty at Alabama A&M University, Dr. Harris held faculty positions at North Carolina Central University in Durham, NC and Cornell University in Ithaca, NY. She earned her bachelor's degree in Business Administration with a concentration in marketing from The American University in Washington, DC. She holds an MBA with course emphases in marketing and finance from Duke University's Fuqua School of Business in Durham, NC, and a PhD in Business Administration from The George Washington University in Washington, DC. Before completing her doctoral program, she taught at various institutions in the greater Washington, DC metropolitan area, including: Howard University, Johns Hopkins University and The George Washington University.

She has received numerous honors during her professional career including North Carolina Central University's Teaching Excellence Award. She has held memberships in a variety of professional organizations including the American Marketing Association, the Atlantic

Marketing Association, and the Academy of Marketing Science, and is a life member of the National Black MBA Association, where she has held a number of leadership positions. Very important to her as well, is her membership in Delta Sigma Theta Sorority, Inc., where she has also held a number of leadership positions.

Dr. Harris acknowledges that exceptional love and support from her family, and an extraordinary network of friends, supporters, and special colleagues, are key ingredients in her professional accomplishments and overall happiness in her life.